Managerial Economics

Managerial Economics

Concepts and Principles

Donald N. Stengel

California State University, Fresno

Managerial Economics: Concepts and Principles
Copyright © Business Expert Press, LLC, 2011.

First published in 2011 by
Business Expert Press, LLC
222 East 46th Street, New York, NY 10017
www.businessexpertpress.com

ISBN-13: 978-1-60649-219-2 (paperback)

ISBN-13: 978-1-60649-220-8 (e-book)

DOI 10.4128/9781606492208

A publication in the Business Expert Press Managerial Economics collection

Collection ISSN: Forthcoming (print)
Collection ISSN: Forthcoming (electronic)

Cover design by Jonathan Pennell
Interior design by Scribe Inc.

First edition: June 2011

10 9 8 7 6 5 4 3 2 1

Printed in the United States of America.

Abstract

Economic principles inform good business decision making. Although economics is sometimes dismissed as a discourse of practical relevance to only a relatively small circle of academicians and policy analysts who call themselves economists, sound economic reasoning benefits any manager of a business, whether they are involved with production and operations, marketing, finance, or corporate strategy. Along with enhancing decision making, the field of economics provides a common language and framework for comprehending and communicating phenomena that occur within a business, as well as between a business and its environment.

This text addresses the core of a subject commonly called managerial economics, which is the application of microeconomics to business decisions. Key relationships between price, quantity, cost, revenue, and profit for an individual firm are presented in the form of simple conceptual models. The text includes key elements from the economics of consumer demand and the economics of production. The book discusses economic motivations for expanding a business and contributions from economics for improved organization of large firms. Market price-quantity equilibrium, competitive behavior, and the role of market structure on market equilibrium and competition are addressed. Finally, the text considers market regulation in terms of the generic problems that create the need for regulation and possible remedies for those problems.

Although the academic literature of managerial economics often employs abstract mathematics and large corporations create and use sophisticated mathematical models that apply economics, this book focuses on concepts, terminology, and principles, with minimal use of mathematics. The reader will gain a better understanding of why businesses and markets function as they do and how those institutions can function better.

Keywords

economics of demand, economics of the firm, economics of organization, economics of production, economics of strategy, market regulation, market structure

Contents

CHAPTER 1

Introduction to Managerial Economics

What Is Managerial Economics?

One standard definition for economics is the study of the production, distribution, and consumption of goods and services. A second definition is the study of choice related to the allocation of scarce resources. The first definition indicates that economics includes any business, nonprofit organization, or administrative unit. The second definition establishes that economics is at the core of what managers of these organizations do.

This book presents economic concepts and principles from the perspective of "managerial economics," which is a subfield of economics that places special emphasis on the choice aspect in the second definition. The purpose of managerial economics is to provide economic terminology and reasoning for the improvement of managerial decisions.

Most readers will be familiar with two different conceptual approaches to the study of economics: microeconomics and macroeconomics. Microeconomics studies phenomena related to goods and services from the perspective of individual decision-making entities—that is, households and businesses. Macroeconomics approaches the same phenomena at an aggregate level, for example, the total consumption and production of a region. Microeconomics and macroeconomics each have their merits. The microeconomic approach is essential for understanding the behavior of atomic entities in an economy. However, understanding the systematic interaction of the many households and businesses would be too complex to derive from descriptions of the individual units. The macroeconomic approach provides measures and theories to understand the overall systematic behavior of an economy.

Since the purpose of managerial economics is to apply economics for the improvement of managerial decisions in an organization, most of the subject material in managerial economics has a microeconomic focus. However, since managers must consider the state of their environment in making decisions and the environment includes the overall economy, an understanding of how to interpret and forecast macroeconomic measures is useful in making managerial decisions.

Why Managerial Economics Is Relevant for Managers

In a civilized society, we rely on others in the society to produce and distribute nearly all the goods and services we need. However, the sources of those goods and services are usually not other individuals but organizations created for the explicit purpose of producing and distributing goods and services. Nearly every organization in our society—whether it is a business, nonprofit entity, or governmental unit—can be viewed as providing a set of goods, services, or both. The responsibility for overseeing and making decisions for these organizations is the role of executives and managers.

Most readers will readily acknowledge that the subject matter of economics applies to their organizations and to their roles as managers. However, some readers may question whether their own understanding of economics is essential, just as they may recognize that physical sciences like chemistry and physics are at work in their lives but have determined they can function successfully without a deep understanding of those subjects.

Whether or not the readers are skeptical about the need to study and understand economics per se, most will recognize the value of studying applied business disciplines like marketing, production/operations management, finance, and business strategy. These subjects form the core of the curriculum for most academic business and management programs, and most managers can readily describe their role in their organization in terms of one or more of these applied subjects. A careful examination of the literature for any of these subjects will reveal that economics provides key terminology and a theoretical foundation. Although we can apply techniques from marketing, production/operations management, and finance without understanding the underlying economics, anyone who wants to understand the why and how behind the technique needs to appreciate the economic rationale for the technique.

We live in a world with scarce resources, which is why economics is a practical science. We cannot have everything we want. Further, others want the same scarce resources we want. Organizations that provide goods and services will survive and thrive only if they meet the needs for which they were created and do so effectively. Since the organization's customers also have limited resources, they will not allocate their scarce resources to acquire something of little or no value. And even if the goods or services are of value, when another organization can meet the same need with a more favorable exchange for the customer, the customer will shift to the other supplier. Put another way, the organization must create value for their customers, which is the difference between what they acquire and what they produce. The thesis of this book is that those managers who understand economics have a competitive advantage in creating value.

Managerial Economics Is Applicable to Different Types of Organizations

In this book, the organization providing goods and services will often be called a "business" or a "firm," terms that connote a for-profit organization. And in some portions of the book, we discuss principles that presume the underlying goal of the organization is to create profit. However, managerial economics is relevant to nonprofit organizations and government agencies as well as conventional, for-profit businesses. Although the underlying objective may change based on the type of organization, all these organizational types exist for the purpose of creating goods or services for persons or other organizations.

Managerial economics also addresses another class of manager: the regulator. As we will discuss in the final chapter, the economic exchanges that result from organizations and persons trying to achieve their individual objectives may not result in the best overall pattern of exchange unless there is some regulatory guidance. Economics provides a framework for analyzing regulation, both the effect on decision making by the regulated entities and the policy decisions of the regulator.

The Focus of This Book

The intent of this book is to familiarize the reader with the key concepts, terminology, and principles from managerial economics. After reading the text, you should have a richer appreciation of your environment—your customers, your suppliers, your competitors, and your regulators. You will learn principles that should improve your intuition and your managerial decisions. You will also be able to communicate more effectively with your colleagues and with expert consultants.

As with much of microeconomic theory, many of the economic principles in this book were originally derived with the help of mathematics and abstract models based on logic and algebra. In this book, the focus is on the insights gained from these principles, not the derivation of the principles, so only a modest level of mathematics is employed here and an understanding of basic algebra will suffice. We will consider some key economic models of managerial decision making, but these will be presented either verbally, graphically, or with simple mathematical representations. For readers who are interested in a more rigorous treatment, the reference list at the conclusion of this text includes several books that will provide more detail. Alternatively, a web search using one of the terms from this book will generally yield several useful links for further exploration of a concept.

A note about economic models is that models are simplified representations of a real-world organization and its environment. Some aspects of the real-world setting are not addressed, and even those aspects that are addressed are simplifications of any actual setting being represented. The point of using models is not to match the actual setting in every detail, but to capture the essential aspects so determinations can be made quickly and with a modest cost. Models are effective when they help us understand the complex and uncertain environment and proceed to appropriate action.

How to Read This Book

Like any academic subject, economics can seem like an abstract pursuit that is of greatest interest to economists who want to communicate with other economists. However, while there is certainly a substantial body of written research that may reinforce that impression, this book is written with the belief that economics provides a language and a perspective that is useful for general managers.

All readers have a considerable experience base with the phenomena that economics tries to address, as managers, consumers, or citizens interested in what is happening in their world and why. As you read the book, I encourage you to try to apply the concepts and theories to economic phenomena you have experienced. By doing so, the content of the book will make more sense and you are more likely to apply what you will read here in your future activities as a player in the world of business and economics.

CHAPTER 2

Key Measures and Relationships

A Simple Business Venture

In this chapter we will be covering some of the key measures and relationships of a business operation. To help illustrate these concepts, we will consider the following simple business venture opportunity.

Suppose three students like spending time at the beach. They have pondered whether they could work and live at the beach during their summer break and learned that they could lease a small building by the beach with existing freezer capacity and apply for a local license to sell ice cream bars.

Revenue, Cost, and Profit

Most businesses sell something—either a physical commodity like an ice cream bar or a service like a car repair. In a modern economy, that sale is made in return for money or at least is evaluated in monetary terms. The total monetary value of the goods or services sold is called *revenue*.

Few businesses are able to sell something without incurring expenses to make the sale possible. The collective expenses incurred to generate revenue over a period of time, expressed in terms of monetary value, are the *cost*. Some cost elements are related to the volume of sales; that is, as sales go up, the expenses go up. These costs are called *variable costs*. The cost of raw materials used to make an item of clothing would be an example of a variable cost. Other costs are largely invariant to the volume of sales, at least within a certain range of sales volumes. These costs are called *fixed costs*. The cost of a machine for cutting cloth to make an item of clothing would be a fixed cost.

Businesses are viable on a sustained basis only when the revenue generated by the business generally exceeds the cost incurred in operating the business. The difference between the revenue and cost (found by subtracting the cost from the revenue) is called the *profit*. When costs exceed revenue, there is a negative profit, or *loss*.

The students in our simple venture realize they need to determine whether they can make a profit from a summer ice cream bar business. They met the person who operated an ice cream bar business in this building the previous summer. He told them last summer he charged $1.50 per ice cream bar and sold 36,000 ice cream bars. He said the cost of the ice cream bars—wholesale purchase, delivery, storage, and so on—comes to about $0.30 per bar. He indicated his other main costs—leasing the building, license, local business association fee, and insurance—came to about $16,000.

Based on this limited information, the students could determine a rough estimate of the revenue, costs, and profit they would have if they were to repeat the outcomes for the prior operator. The revenue would be $1.50 per ice cream bar times 36,000 ice cream bars, or $54,000. The variable cost would be $0.30 per ice cream bar times 36,000 ice cream bars, or $10,800. The fixed cost would be $16,000, making the total cost $26,800. The profit would be $54,000 minus $26,800, or $27,200.

Based on this analysis, the students are confident the summer business venture can make money. They approach the owner of the building and learn that if they want to reserve the right of first option to lease the building over the summer, they will need to make a nonrefundable $6000 deposit that will be applied to the lease. They proceeded to make that deposit.

A few weeks later, all three students were unexpectedly offered summer business internships at a large corporation. Each student would earn $10,000. However, the work site for the internships is far from the beach and they would be in an office all day. They now must decide whether to accept the internships and terminate their plan to run a business at the beach or turn down the internships.

Economic Versus Accounting
Measures of Cost and Profit

The discipline of accounting provides guidelines for the measurement of revenue, cost, and profit. Having analyses based on generally accepted principles is important for making exchanges in our economy. For example, corporations must produce financial statements to help investors and creditors assess the health of the corporation. Individuals and businesses must produce tax returns to determine a fair measurement of income for taxation purposes.

Costs as measured according to accounting principles are not necessarily the relevant measurements for decisions related to operating or acquiring a business. For example, accounting standards dictate that businesses depreciate long-lived assets, like buildings, by spreading the cost over the life of the asset.[1] However, from the perspective of the business, the entire expense was incurred when the asset was acquired, even if borrowing was necessary to make the purchase and there will be the opportunity to take increased tax deductions in future years.

Likewise, there are other business costs relevant to decision making that may not be considered as costs from the perspective of accounting standards. For example, the owner/operator of a proprietorship invests time and effort in operating a business. These would typically not be treated as expenses on the proprietorship's tax return but are certainly relevant to the owner in deciding how to manage his self-run business.

Based on these differences in perspective, it is useful to distinguish *accounting costs* from *economic costs*. In turn, since profit is the residue of revenue minus costs, we also distinguish *accounting profit* from *economic profit*.

Consider our three students who are now in a quandary about whether to sell ice cream bars on the beach or accept the summer internships, and let us see how distinguishing the economic cost/profit from the accounting cost/profit helps to clarify their decision.

There is the matter of the students' time and energy, which is not reflected in the projection of the $27,200 profit based on last year's operation. One way to measure that cost is based on how much they will forfeit by not using their time in the next best alternative, which in this case is the summer internship. We can consider this forfeited income as being equivalent to a charge against the operation of the ice cream business, a measurement commonly referred to as an *opportunity cost*. The students' time has an opportunity cost of $30,000. This should be added to the earlier fixed cost of $16,000, making an economic fixed cost of $46,000, a total economic cost of $56,800, and an economic loss of $2800. So maybe the ice cream business would not be a good idea after all.

However, recall that the students have already made a $6000 nonrefundable deposit. This money is spent whether the students proceed to run the summer business or not. It is an example of what is called a *sunk cost*. Assuming the fixed cost of the business was the same as for the prior operator, the students would have a $16,000 accounting fixed cost to report on a tax return. Yet, from the perspective of economic costs, only $10,000 is really still avoidable by not operating the business. The remaining $6000 is gone regardless of what the students decide. So, from an economic cost/profit perspective, viewed after the nonrefundable deposit but before the students declined the summer internships, if the students' other costs and revenue were identical to the previous year, they would have economic costs of just $50,800 and an economic profit of $3200.

If a business properly measures costs from an economic perspective, ignoring sunk costs and including opportunity costs, you can conclude that *a venture is worth pursuing if it results in an economic profit of zero or better*. However, this is generally not a valid principle if you measure performance in terms of accounting profit. Most stockholders in a corporation would not be satisfied if the corporation only managed a zero accounting profit because this means there is no residual from the business to reward them with either dividends or increased stock value. From an economic cost perspective, stockholder capital is an asset that can be redeployed, and thus it has an opportunity cost—namely, what the investor could earn elsewhere with their share of the corporation in a different investment of equivalent risk.[2] This opportunity cost could be estimated and included in the economic cost. If the resulting profit is zero or positive after netting out the opportunity cost of capital, the investor's participation is worthwhile.

Revenue, Cost, and Profit Functions

In the preceding projections for the proposed ice cream bar venture, the assumption was that 36,000 ice cream bars would be sold based on the volume in the prior summer. However, the actual volume for a future venture might be higher or lower. And with an economic profit so close to zero, our students should consider the impact of any such differences.

There is a relationship between the volume or quantity created and sold and the resulting impact on revenue, cost, and profit. These relationships are called the revenue function, cost function, and profit function. These relationships can be expressed in terms of tables, graphs, or algebraic equations.

In a case where a business sells one kind of product or service, revenue is the product of the price per unit times the number of units sold. If we assume ice cream bars will be sold for $1.50 apiece, the equation for the revenue function will be

$$R = \$1.5\ Q,$$

where R is the revenue and Q is the number of units sold.

The cost function for the ice cream bar venture has two components: the fixed cost component of $40,000 that remains the same regardless of the volume of units and the variable cost component of $0.30 times the number of items. The equation for the cost function is

$$C = \$40,000 + \$0.3\ Q,$$

where C is the total cost. Note we are measuring economic cost, not accounting cost.

Since profit is the difference between revenue and cost, the profit functions will be

$$\pi = R - C = \$1.2\ Q - \$40,000.$$

Here π is used as the symbol for profit. (The letter P is reserved for use later as a symbol for price.)

Table 2.1 provides actual values for revenue, cost, and profit for selected values of the volume quantity Q. Figure 2.1 provides graphs of the revenue, cost, and profit functions.

The average cost is another interesting measure to track. This is calculated by dividing the total cost by the quantity. The relationship between average cost and quantity is the *average cost function*. For the ice cream bar venture, the equation for this function would be

$$AC = C/Q = (\$40,000 + \$0.3\ Q)/Q = \$0.3 + \$40,000/Q.$$

Figure 2.2 shows a graph of the average cost function. Note that the average cost function starts out very high but drops quickly and levels off.

Table 2.1. Revenue, Cost, and Profit for Selected Sales Volumes for
Ice Cream Bar Venture

Units	Revenue	Cost	Profit
0	$0	$40,000	–$40,000
10,000	$15,000	$43,000	–$28,000
20,000	$30,000	$46,000	–$16,000
30,000	$45,000	$49,000	–$4,000
40,000	$60,000	$52,000	$8,000
50,000	$75,000	$55,000	$20,000
60,000	$90,000	$58,000	$32,000

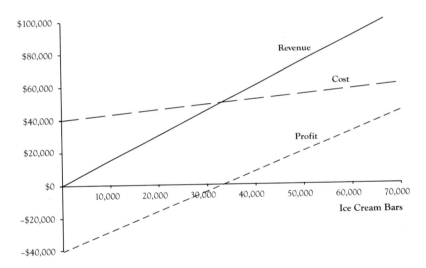

Figure 2.1. Graphs of revenue, cost, and profit functions for ice cream
bar business at price of $1.50.

Essentially the average cost function is the variable cost per unit of $0.30
plus a portion of the fixed cost allocated across all units. For low volumes,
there are few units to spread the fixed cost, so the average cost is very
high. However, as the volume gets large, the fixed cost impact on average
cost becomes small and is dominated by the variable cost component.

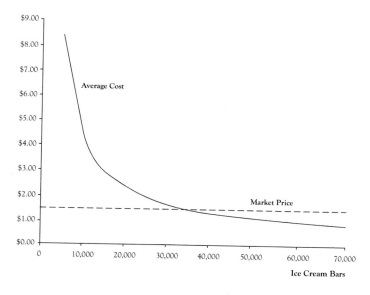

Figure 2.2. Graph of average cost function for ice cream bar venture.

Breakeven Analysis

A scan of Figure 2.1 shows that the ice cream bar venture could result in an economic profit or loss depending on the volume of business. As the sales volume increases, revenue and cost increase and profit becomes progressively less negative, turns positive, and then becomes increasingly positive. There is a zone of lower volume levels where economic costs exceed revenues and a zone on the higher volume levels where revenues exceed economic costs.

One important consideration for our three students is whether they are confident that the sales volume will be high enough to fall in the range of positive economic profits. The volume level that separates the range with economic loss from the range with economic profit is called the *breakeven point*. From the graph we can see the breakeven point is slightly less than 35,000 units. If the students can sell above that level, which the prior operator did, it will be worthwhile to proceed with the venture. If they are doubtful of reaching that level, they should abandon the venture now, even if that means losing their nonrefundable deposit.

There are a number of ways to determine a precise value for the break-even level algebraically. One is to solve for the value of Q that makes the economic profit function equal to zero:

$$0 = \$1.2\,Q - \$40{,}000 \text{ or } Q = \$40{,}000/\$1.2 = 33{,}334 \text{ units.}$$

An equivalent approach is to find the value of Q where the revenue function and cost function have identical values.

Another way to assess the breakeven point is to find how large the volume must be before the average cost drops to the price level. In this case, we need to find the value of Q where AC is equal to $1.50. This occurs at the breakeven level calculated earlier.

A fourth approach to solving for the breakeven level is to consider how profit changes as the volume level increases. Each additional item sold incurs a variable cost per unit of $0.30 and is sold for a price of $1.50. The difference, called the *unit contribution margin*, would be $1.20. For each additional unit of volume, the profit increases by $1.20. In order to make an overall economic profit, the business would need to accrue a sufficient number of unit contribution margins to cover the economic fixed cost of $40,000. So the breakeven level would be

$$Q = \text{fixed cost}/(\text{price per unit} - \text{variable cost per unit})$$
$$= \$40{,}000/(\$1.50 - \$0.30) = 33{,}333.3 \text{ or } 33{,}334 \text{ units.}$$

Once the operating volume crosses the breakeven threshold, each additional unit contribution margin results in additional profit.

We get an interesting insight into the nature of a business by comparing the unit contribution margin with the price. In the case of the ice cream business, the unit contribution margin is 80% of the price. When the price and unit contribution margins are close, most of the revenue generated from additional sales turns into profit once you get above the breakeven level. However, if you fall below the breakeven level, the loss will grow equally dramatically as the volume level drops. Businesses like software providers, which tend have mostly fixed costs, see a close correlation between revenue and profit. Businesses of this type tend to be high risk and high reward.

On the other hand, businesses that have predominantly variable costs, such as a retail grocery outlet, tend to have relatively modest changes in profit relative to changes in revenue. If business level falls off, they can scale down their variable costs and profit will not decline so much. At the same time, large increases in volume levels beyond the breakeven level can achieve only modest profit gains because most of the additional revenue is offset by additional variable costs.

The Impact of Price Changes

In the preceding analyses of the ice cream venture, we assumed ice cream bars would be priced at $1.50 per unit based on the price that was charged in the previous summer. The students can change the price and should evaluate whether there is a better price for them to charge. However, if the price is lowered, the breakeven level will increase and if the price is raised, the breakeven level will drop, but then so may the customer demand.

To examine the impact of price and determine a best price, we need to estimate the relationship between the price charged and the maximum unit quantity that could be sold. This relationship is called a *demand curve*. Demand curves generally follow a pattern called the *law of demand*, whereby increases in price result in decreases in the maximum quantity that can be sold.

We will consider a simple demand curve for the ice cream venture. We will assume that since the operator of the business last year sold 36,000 units at a price of $1.50 that we could sell up to 36,000 units at the same price this coming summer. Next, suppose the students had asked the prior operator how many ice cream bars he believes he would have sold at a price of $2.00 and the prior operator responds that he probably would have sold 10,000 fewer ice cream bars. In other words, he estimates his sales would have been 26,000 at a price of $2.00 per ice cream bar.

To develop a demand curve from the prior operator's estimates, the students assume that the relationship between price and quantity is linear, meaning that the change in quantity will be proportional to the change in price. Graphically, you can infer this relationship by plotting the two price-quantity pairs on a graph and connecting them with a straight line. Using intermediate algebra, you can derive an equation for the linear demand curve

$$P = 3.3 - 0.00005\ Q,$$

where P is price in dollars and Q is the maximum number of ice cream bars that will sell at this price. Figure 2.3 presents a graph of the demand curve.

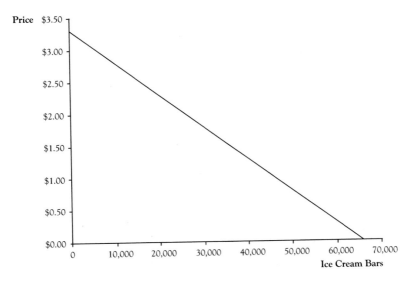

Figure 2.3. Linear demand curve for ice cream bar venture.

It may seem awkward to express the demand curve in a manner that you use the quantity Q to solve for the price P. After all, in a fixed price market, the seller decides a price and the buyers respond with the volume of demand. Mathematically, the relationship for ice cream bars could be written

$$Q = 66,000 - 20,000 \text{ P.}$$

However, in economics, the common practice is to describe the demand curve as the highest price that could be charged and still sell a quantity Q.

The linear demand curve in Figure 2.3 probably stretches credibility as you move to points where either the price is zero or demand is zero. In actuality, demand curves are usually curved such that demand will get very high as the price approaches zero and small amounts would still sell at very high prices, similar to the pattern in Figure 2.4. However, linear demand curves can be reasonably good estimates of behavior if they are used within limited zone of possible prices.

We can use the stated relationship in the demand curve to examine the impact of price changes on the revenue and profit functions. (The cost function is unaffected by the demand curve.) Again, with a single type of product or service, revenue is equal to price times quantity. By

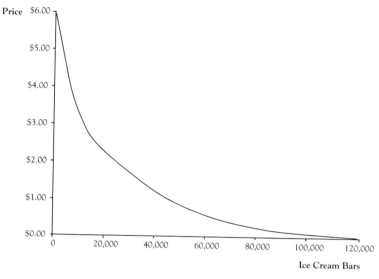

Figure 2.4. Common pattern for demand curves.

using the expression for price in terms of quantity rather than a fixed price, we can find the resulting revenue function

$$R = P\,Q = (3.3 - 0.00005\,Q)\,Q = 3.3\,Q - 0.00005\,Q^2.$$

By subtracting the expression for the cost function from the revenue function, we get the revised profit function

$$\pi = (3.3\,Q - 0.00005\,Q^2) - (40{,}000 + \$0.3\,Q)$$
$$= -0.00005\,Q^2 + 3\,Q - 40{,}000.$$

Graphs for the revised revenue, cost, and profit functions appear in Figure 2.5. Note that the revenue and profit functions are curved since they are quadratic functions. From the graph of the profit function, it can be seen that it is possible to earn an economic profit with a quantity as low as 20,000 units; however, the price would need to be increased according to the demand curve for this profit to materialize. Additionally, it appears a higher profit is possible than at the previously planned operation of 36,000 units at a price of $1.50. The highest profitability appears to be at a volume of about 30,000 units. The presumed price at this volume based on the demand curve would be around $1.80.

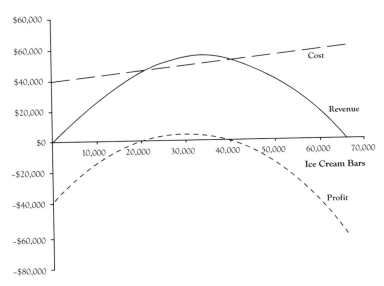

Figure 2.5. Graphs of revenue, cost, and profit functions for ice cream bar venture for linear demand curve.

Marginal Analysis

Economists analyze relationships like revenue functions from the perspective of how the function changes in response to a small change in the quantity. These marginal measurements not only provide a numerical value to the responsiveness of the function to changes in the quantity but also can indicate whether the business would benefit from increasing or decreasing the planned production volume and in some cases can even help determine the optimal level of planned production.

The *marginal revenue* measures the change in revenue in response to a unit increase in production level or quantity. The *marginal cost* measures the change in cost corresponding to a unit increase in the production level. The *marginal profit* measures the change in profit resulting from a unit increase in the quantity. Marginal measures for economic functions are related to the operating volume and may change if assessed at a different operating volume level.

There are multiple computational techniques for actually calculating these marginal measures. If the relationships have been expressed in the form of algebraic equations, one approach is to evaluate the function at the quantity level of interest, evaluate the function if the quantity level is increased by one, and determine the change from the first value to the second.

Suppose we want to evaluate the marginal revenue for the revenue function derived in the previous section at last summer's operating level of 36,000 ice cream bars. For a value of Q = 36,000, the revenue function returns a value of $54,000. For a value of Q = 36,001, the revenue function returns a value of $53,999.70. So, with this approach, the marginal revenue would be $53,999.70 – $54,000, or –$0.30. What does this tell us? First, it tells us that for a modest increase in production volume, if we adjust the price downward to compensate for the increase in quantity, the net change in revenue is a decrease of $0.30 for each additional unit of planned production.

Marginal measures often can be used to assess the change if quantity is decreased by changing sign on the marginal measure. Thus, if the marginal revenue is –$0.30 at Q = 36,000, we can estimate that for modest decreases in planned quantity level (and adjustment of the price upward based on the demand function), revenue will rise $0.30 per unit of decrease in Q.

At first glance, the fact that a higher production volume can result in lower revenue seems counterintuitive, if not flawed. After all, if you sell more and are still getting a positive price, how can more volume result in less revenue? What is happening in this illustrated instance is that the price drop, as a percentage of the price, exceeds the increase in quantity as a percentage of quantity. A glance back at Figure 2.5 confirms that Q = 36,000 is in the portion of the revenue function where the revenue function declines as quantity gets larger.

If you follow the same computational approach to calculate the marginal cost and marginal profit when Q = 36,000, you would find that the marginal cost is $0.30 and the marginal profit is –$0.60. Note that marginal profit is equal to marginal revenue minus marginal cost, which will always be the case.

The marginal cost of $0.30 is the same as the variable cost of acquiring and stocking an ice cream bar. This is not just a coincidence. If you have a cost function that takes the form of a linear equation, marginal cost will always equal the variable cost per unit.

The fact that marginal profit is negative at Q = 36,000 indicates we can expect to find a more profitable value by decreasing the quantity and increasing the price, but not by increasing the quantity and decreasing the price. The marginal profit value does not provide enough information to tell us how much to lower the planned quantity, but like a compass, it points us in the right direction.

Since marginal measures are the rate of change in the function value corresponding to a modest change in Q, differential calculus provides another computational technique for deriving marginal measures. Differential calculus finds *instantaneous* rates of change, so the values computed are based on infinitesimal changes in Q rather than whole units of Q and thus can yield slightly different values. However, a great strength of using differential calculus is that whenever you have an economic function in the form of an algebraic equation, you can use differential calculus to derive an entire function that can be used to calculate the marginal value at *any* value of Q.

How to apply differential calculus is beyond the scope of this text; however, here are the functions that can be derived from the revenue, cost, and profit functions of the previous section (i.e., those that assume a variable price related to quantity):

$$\text{marginal revenue at a volume } Q = \$3.3 - \$0.0001\,Q,$$

$$\text{marginal cost at a volume } Q = \$\,0.3,$$

$$\text{marginal profit at a volume } Q = \$3 - \$0.0001\,Q.$$

Substituting Q = 36,000 into these equations will produce the same values we found earlier. However, these marginal functions are capable of more.

Since the marginal change in the function is the rate of change in the function at a particular point, you can visualize this by looking at the graphs of the functions and drawing a tangent line on the graph at the quantity level of interest. A tangent line is a straight line that goes through the point on the graph, but does not cross the graph as it goes through the point. The slope of the tangent line is the marginal value of the function at that point. When the slope is upward (the tangent line rises as it goes to the right), the marginal measure will be positive. When the slope is downward, the marginal measure will be negative. If the line has a steep slope, the magnitude of the marginal measure will be large. When the line is fairly flat, the magnitude will be small.

Suppose we want to find where the profit function is at its highest value. If you look at that point (in the vicinity of Q = 30,000) on Figure 2.5, you see it is like being on the top of a hill. If you draw the tangent line, it will not be sloped upward or downward; it will be a flat line with a zero slope. This means the marginal profit at the quantity with the highest profit has a value of zero. So if you set the marginal profit function equal to zero and solve for Q you find

$$0 = \$3.00 - \$0.0001 \, Q \text{ implies } Q = \$3.00/\$0.0001 = 30,000.$$

This confirms our visual location of the optimum level and provides a precise value.

This example illustrates a general economic principle: Unless there is a constraint preventing a change to a more profitable production level, the most profitable production level will be at a level where marginal profit equals zero. Equivalently, in the absence of production level constraints, the most profitable production level is where marginal revenue is equal to marginal cost. If marginal revenue is greater than marginal cost at some production level and the level can be increased, profit will increase by doing so. If marginal cost is greater than marginal revenue and the production level can be decreased, again the profit can be increased.

The Conclusion for Our Students

Our students will look at this analysis and decide not only to go forward with the ice cream business on the beach but to charge $1.80, since that is the price on the demand curve corresponding to a sales volume of 30,000 ice cream bars. Their expected revenue will be $54,000, which coincidently is the same as in the original plan, but the economic costs will be only $49,000, which is lower than in the original analysis, and their economic profit will be slightly higher, at $5000.

At first glance, a $5000 profit does not seem like much. However, bear in mind that we already assigned an opportunity cost to the students' time based on the income foregone by not accepting the corporate internships. So the students can expect to complete the summer with $10,000 each to compensate for the lost internship income and still have an additional $5000 to split between them.

The Shutdown Rule

You may recall earlier in this chapter that, before deciding to disregard the $6000 nonrefundable down payment (to hold the option to operate the ice cream business) as a relevant economic cost, the total cost of operating the business under a plan to sell 36,000 ice cream bars at a price of $1.50 per item would have exceeded the expected revenue. Even after further analysis indicated that the students could improve profit by planning to sell 30,000 ice cream bars at a price of $1.80 each, if the $6000 deposit had not been a sunk cost, there would have been no planned production level and associated price on the demand curve that would have resulted in positive economic profit. So the students would have determined the ice cream venture to be not quite viable if they had known prior to making the deposit that they could instead each have a summer corporate internship. However, having committed the $6000 deposit already, they will gain going forward by proceeding to run the ice cream bar business.

A similar situation can occur in ongoing business concerns. A struggling business may appear to generate insufficient revenue to cover costs yet continue to operate, at least for a while. Such a practice may be rational when a sizeable portion of the fixed costs in the near term are effectively sunk, and the revenue generated is enough to offset the remaining fixed costs and variable costs that are still not firmly committed.

Earlier in the chapter, we cited one condition for reaching a breakeven production level where revenue would equal or exceed costs as the point where average cost per unit is equal to the price. However, if some of the costs are already sunk, these should be disregarded in determining the relevant average cost. In a circumstance where a business regards all fixed costs as effectively sunk for the next production period, this condition becomes a statement of a principle known as the *shutdown rule*: If the selling price per unit is at least as large as the average variable cost per unit, the firm should continue to operate for at least a while; otherwise, the firm would be better to shut down operations immediately.

Two observations about the shutdown rule are in order: In a circumstance where a firm's revenue is sufficient to meet variable costs but not total costs (including the sunk costs), although the firm may operate for a period of time because the additional revenue generated will cover the additional costs, eventually the fixed costs will need to be refreshed and those will be relevant economic costs prior to commitment to continue operating beyond the near term. If a business does not see circumstances changing whereby revenue will be getting better or costs will be going down, although it may be a net gain to operate for some additional time, such a firm should eventually decide to close down its business.

Sometimes, it is appropriate to shut down a business for a period of time, but not to close the business permanently. This may happen if temporary unfavorable circumstances mean even uncommitted costs cannot be covered by revenue in the near term, but the business expects favorable conditions to resume later. An example of this would be the owner of an oil drilling operation. If crude oil prices drop very low, the operator may be unable to cover variable costs and it would be best to shut down until petroleum prices climb back and operations will be profitable again. In other cases, the opportunity cost of resources may be temporarily high, so the economic profit is negative even if the accounting profit would be positive. An example would be a farmer selling his water rights for the upcoming season because he is offered more for the water rights than he could net using the water and farming.

A Final Word on Business Objectives

In the example used in this chapter, we assumed the students' goal in how to operate the ice cream business was to maximize their profit—more specifically, to maximize their economic profit. Is this an appropriate overall objective for most businesses?

Generally speaking, the answer is yes. If a business is not able to generate enough revenue to at least cover their economic costs, the business is losing in the net. In addition to the business owners having to cover the loss out of their wealth (or out of society's largesse for a bankruptcy), there is an inefficiency from a societal perspective in that the resources used by the business could be more productive elsewhere.

The ice cream business analyzed here was simple in many respects, including that it was intended to operate for only a short period of time. Most businesses are intended to operate for long periods of time. Some businesses, especially newly formed businesses, will intentionally operate businesses at a loss or operate at volumes higher than would generate the maximum profit in the next production period. This decision is rational if the business expects to realize larger profits in future periods in exchange for enduring a loss in the near future. There are quantitative techniques, such as discounting,[3] that allow a business decision maker to make these trade-offs between profit now and profit later. These techniques will not be covered in this text.

Economists refer to a measure called *the value of the firm*, which is the collective value of all economic profits into the future and approximately the amount the owners should expect to receive if they sold the business to a different set of owners. For a corporation, in theory this would roughly equate to the value of the equity on a company's balance sheet, although due to several factors like sunk costs, is probably not really that value. Economists would say that a business should make decisions that maximize the value of the firm, meaning the best decisions will result in larger economic profits either now or later.

One response to the principle that the overall goal of a firm is to maximize its value is that, although that goal may be best for those who own the business, it is not the optimal objective for the overall society in which the business operates. One specific objection is that those who work for the business may not be the same as those who own the business and maximizing the value for the owners can mean exploiting the nonowner employees. The common response to this objection is that it will be in the owners' best interest in the long run (several periods of operation) to treat their employees fairly. Businesses that exploit their employees will lose their good employees and fail to motivate those employees who remain. The collective result will be lower profits and a lower value of the firm.

A second objection to the appropriateness of operating a business to maximize the value for the owners is that this invites businesses to exploit their customers, suppliers, and the society in which they operate to make more money. Firms may be able to take advantage of outside parties for a while, but eventually the customers and suppliers will wise up and stop interacting with the business. With a high level of distrust, there will be a decline in profits in future periods that will more than offset any immediate gain. If a business tries to exploit the overall society by ruining the environment or causing an increase in costs to the public, the business can expect governmental authorities to take actions to punish the firm or limit its operations, again resulting in a net loss over time. So maximizing the value of the firm for the owners does not imply more profit for the owners at the expense of everyone else. Rather, a rational pursuit of maximal value will respect the other stakeholders of a business.

In the case of nonprofit organizations, maximizing the value of the organization will be different than with for-profit businesses like our ice cream example. A nonprofit organization may be given a budget that sets an upper limit on its costs and is expected to provide the most value to the people it serves. Since most nonprofit organizations do not charge their "customers" in the same way as for-profit businesses, the determination of value will be different than estimating sales revenue. Techniques such as cost-benefit analysis[4] have been developed for this purpose.

CHAPTER 3

Demand and Pricing

Decisions related to demand and pricing are usually called marketing decisions. Marketing is an established profession and an applied academic discipline with a large body of literature. However, economic reasoning and concepts provide much of the theoretical foundation for marketing practice. In this chapter, we will address these elements from the perspective of economics.

Theory of the Consumer

Back in chapter 2, we used a demand curve to represent the relationship between the price charged for ice cream bars and the maximum number of ice cream bars that customers would purchase. We will address how to create a demand curve later in this chapter, but we will begin our discussion with a brief review of microeconomic theory that endeavors to explain how consumers behave.

A consumer is someone who makes consumption decisions for herself or for her household unit. In a modern society, consumption is largely facilitated by purchases for goods and services. Some of these goods and services are essential to a consumer's livelihood, but others are discretionary, perhaps even a luxury. Consumers are limited in how much they can consume by their wealth. A consumer's wealth will change over time due to income and expenditures. She might be able to borrow against future income so as to increase her capacity to purchase now in exchange for diminished wealth and consumption later. Similarly, she may retain some of her current wealth as savings toward increased future consumption. Consumption decisions may be planned into the future, taking account of the expected changes in wealth over time.

The theory of the consumer posits that a consumer plans her purchases, the timing of those purchases, and borrowing and saving so as maximize the satisfaction she and her household unit will experience from consumption of goods and services. In this theory, consumers are able to compare any two patterns of consumption, borrowing, and saving and deem that either one is preferred to the second or they are indifferent between the two patterns. Based on the ability to do these comparisons, consumers look at the prices charged for various services now, and what they expect prices to be for goods and services in the future, and select the pattern of consumption, borrowing, and saving that generates the greatest satisfaction over their lifetime within the constraint of their wealth and expected future income.

Although the consumers may anticipate changes in prices over time, they may find that their guesses about future prices are incorrect. When this happens, the theory states that they will adjust their consumption, borrowing, and saving to restore the optimality under the newly revealed prices. In fact, the theory identifies two effects of price changes: the substitution effect and the income effect.

The *substitution* effect is based on an argument employing marginal reasoning like the marginal analysis discussed in chapter 2. Economists often use the term *utility* as a hypothetical quantitative value for satisfaction that a consumer receives from a pattern of consumption. If a consumer were to receive one more unit of some good or service, the resulting increase in their utility is called the *marginal utility of the good*. As a consequence of maximizing their overall satisfaction from consumption, or equivalently maximizing their utility, it will be the case that if you take the marginal utility of one good or service and divide it by its price, you should get the same ratio for any other good or service. If they were not roughly equal, the consumer would be able to swap consumption of one good or service for another, keep within their wealth constraint, and have higher utility. The substitution effect is the consumer's response to a changing price to restore balance in the ratios of marginal utility to price.

Just as a simple illustration, suppose a consumer likes bananas and peaches as a treat. For the sake of the illustration, let's suppose an additional banana has a marginal utility of 2 and a peach has a marginal utility of 3. If a banana costs $0.20 and a peach costs $0.30, bananas and peaches have a ratio of the marginal utility to its price equal to 10. If the peach price increases to $0.40, the ratio will become lower for peaches and the consumer may substitute some purchases of peaches with purchases of more bananas.

As the result of price changes and substitution, the consumer's overall utility may increase or decrease. Consequently, the consumer may experience the equivalent of an increase or decrease in wealth, in the sense that it would have required a different level of wealth to just barely afford the new consumption pattern under the previous set of prices. This equivalent change in purchasing power is called the *income effect*.

Economists have precise techniques for separating the response to a price change into a substitution effect and an income effect.[1] This is beyond the scope of this text. For our purposes, it is sufficient to appreciate that price changes will affect the mix of goods and services that is best and change the consumer's overall level of satisfaction.

In most cases, the primary response to a price change is a substitution effect, with a relatively modest income effect. However, for goods and services that a consumer cannot substitute easily, a sizeable price change may have a significant income effect. For example, when gasoline prices jumped dramatically in the United States, consumers may have reduced their driving somewhat but were unable to find a substitute for the essential needs served by driving their cars. As a result, consumers experienced a dramatic drop in wealth available for other goods and services and consumed generally less of all of those to compensate for the greater expenditure on gasoline.

Normally, price increases result in less consumption of the associated good or service, whereas price decreases results in more consumption. This typical pattern is usually supported by both the substitution effect and the income effect. An interesting exception is the case of *Giffen goods*, which is a situation where consumption of a good or service may increase in response to a price increase or decrease in response to a price decrease. This anomaly is explained by a strong income effect. An economist named Robert Giffen discovered that Irish consumers increased the use of potatoes in their diet during the Irish Potato Famine of the 1840s, even though the price of potatoes rose dramatically. Basically, because potatoes were a staple of the Irish diet, when the potato price increased, the wealth available to purchase other food items diminished and Irish consumers wanted to purchase more potatoes to compensate for the diminished purchases of other food items.

Is the Theory of the Consumer Realistic?

Strictly speaking, it would be difficult to make a case that the theory of the consumer conforms to our own experience of consumption decisions or what we observe of other consumers. We don't consciously weigh the relative marginal utilities of tens of thousands of possible goods and services we might consume. We don't know all the current prices and don't even know of the existence of many goods and services. Even if we did, the computational complexity to solve for optimal consumption would overwhelm our faculties, and probably even the fastest computers available.

Many times we and others don't think of our consumption in terms of what gives us the greatest satisfaction but in terms of what it takes to get by. Consumers who are impoverished or suffer a major ailment are probably unable to do even a modest attempt at optimizing consumption. Others may simply consume as a matter of habit rather than conscious choice.

Although our consumption decisions may not fully conform to the theory of the consumer, there have been some attempts to argue that we do approximate it. Herbert Simon proposed a theory of bounded rationality[2] that states that humans do behave rationally with a limited range of options. So if consumers focus on a modest set of important goods and services, they may be able to achieve something close to the theoretical optimum in terms of overall utility. Simon also observed that human beings may not optimize so much as they "satisfice," meaning that they work to meet a certain level of consumption satisfaction rather than the very best pattern of consumption. If the level of acceptability is reasonably close to the optimum level, again the results of consumption decisions may approximate what would occur if the consumers operated according to this theory.

Another argument suggesting that differences between the theory and actual behavior may not result in starkly different consumption is that we observe how others behave. If someone else, either by active choice or by accidental discovery, is experiencing greater satisfaction under similar circumstances of wealth and income, their friends and neighbors will detect it and start to emulate their consumption patterns. So our consumption may evolve in the direction of the optimal pattern.

Perhaps most importantly, the lack of face validity of the theory of the consumer does mean the theory is not useful in modeling consumer behavior. We do expect consumers to respond to price changes and we do expect consumers to respond to changes in their wealth, whether due to changes in their actual discretionary income or indirect impacts on wealth resulting from price changes.

Determinants of Demand

We can approach the challenge of modeling consumer behavior in a more practical manner that is informed by the theory of the consumer. To estimate demand and study the nature of consumer demand, we start by identifying a set of key factors that have a strong influence on consumer demand.

Probably the most important influencing factor is one we considered for the ice cream business in chapter 2—the price of the item itself. Price is also the key determinant of demand in the theory of the consumer. In the simplest cases, there is a single price that applies to any item or unit of service being sold. However, as we will discuss later in the section on price discrimination, prices may vary depending on who is buying it and how much they are buying.

Businesses incur promotional costs to boost the consumption of their products. Promotion can be in the form of advertising, free samples, appearance in business directories, and so on. The theory of the consumer provides a supporting rationale for expenditure on promotion: If a consumer is regarded as deciding how to allocate his wealth across available goods and services, in order for your product to be included as a candidate in that choice, the consumer has to be aware that your product or service exists. However, as we will discuss in chapter 7, large firms often engage in promotion at expenditure levels well beyond what is needed to make your firm and product known to the consumer, as a tactic of competition.

Consumer demand may vary depending on where and when the consumption is occurring. Being able to quantitatively assess how consumption changes by location or time is a powerful tool in deciding where and when to sell your product. Some businesses decide to serve broad geographical regions; others target specific locations. Some businesses sell most or all times of the day and days of the year; others limit their operations to a restricted number of hours or periods within a year. What strategy will work best will depend on the product and the company's overall marketing strategy.

Businesses have a choice of channels for selling. They can operate their own commercial establishments or sell wholesale to other retailers. Goods can be sold directly at a retail site or via the Internet, telephone, or mail order. Understanding how the channels used will affect demand is important.

The selection of price, promotional activities, location, and channel are generally in the control of the business concern. In texts on marketing strategy,[3] the composition of these decisions is called a *marketing mix*. For a marketing mix to be effective, the different elements need to be consistent.

However, there are other important determinants of consumption for a good or service that are largely out of the control of the providing firm. We will next consider some of these determinants.

As suggested by the substitution effect in the theory of the consumer, the consumer is able to alter his pattern of consumption to meet his needs as prices and wealth levels change. The most significant swaps are likely to be between goods and services that come close to meeting the same consumer need. For example, a banana can serve as a substitute for a peach in meeting the need for a piece of fruit. Usually the items that act as substitutes to the product of one firm will be sold by a different firm. Consequently, how that other firm elects to price, promote, locate, and channel its goods or services will have an impact on the consumption of substitutable goods or services sold by the first firm.

Different goods and services can be strongly related in another way called a complementary relationship. Consumption of some goods and services can necessitate greater consumption of other goods and services. For example, if more automobiles are sold, there will be increased demand for tires, oil, repair services, automobile financing, automobile insurance, and so on. Correctly monitoring and forecasting the demand of key complements can improve the ability of a firm to forecast its own consumer demand.

Most firms sell multiple products and services that are related. Within this collection, there are probably important substitute and complementary relationships. A car dealer that sells several models of vehicles has substitutable products that compete with each other. The car dealer may be offering services like repair service and financing that are complementary to vehicle sales. In situations with strong substitute and complementary product relationships, the firm needs to consider these in its demand forecasting and market strategy.

Earlier, we discussed the income effect caused by price changes and indicated that this is caused by the consumer realizing an increase or decrease in overall purchasing wealth. Probably a more significant cause of changes in wealth occurs from fluctuations in the economic activity, which will affect the demand for most goods and services. The relationship between demand quantities and economic indicators of economic activity or disposable income can improve business forecasting considerably.

Demand is also affected by the demographics of the population of eligible customers. How many people live in a region, their ethnic and socioeconomic composition, and age distribution can explain variations in demand across regions and the ability to forecast in the future as these demographics change.

Modeling Consumer Demand

To develop a formal model of consumer demand, the first step is to identify the most important determinants of demand and define variables that measure those determinants. Ideally, we should use variables for which data exist so that statistical estimation techniques can be applied to develop an algebraic relationship between the units of a good consumed and the values of the key determinants. Techniques to derive these algebraic relationships from historical data are outside the scope of this text, but an interested reader may want to consult a text on econometrics.[4]

We will examine a simple example of a model of consumer demand. Suppose a business is selling broadband services in a community. The managers of the business have identified four key determinants of demand: (a) the price they charge for the service, (b) their advertising expenditure, (c) the price charged by the competition, and (d) the disposable income of their potential customers. They define four variables to measure these determinants:

P = the price per month of their service, in dollars,

A = advertising expenditure per month, in dollars,

CP = the price per month of the competitor's service, in dollars,

DIPC = the disposable income per capita, in dollars, as measured by the U.S. Department of Commerce for that month.

Using past data, they estimate the following equation to relate these variables to number of broadband subscribers to their service during a month, symbolized by Q:

$$Q = 25{,}800 - 800\,P + 4\,A + 200\,CP + 0.4\,DIPC.$$

This relationship is called a *demand function.*

One application of the demand function is to estimate the consumption quantity Q for specific values of P, CP, and DIPC. Suppose P = \$30, A = \$5000, CP = \$25, and DIPC = \$33,000:

$$Q = 25{,}800 - 800(30) + 4(5000) + 200(25) + 0.4(33{,}000)$$
$$= 40{,}000 \text{ subscribers}$$

In chapter 2, we introduced a demand curve to describe the relationship between the quantity of items sold and the price of the item. When there are multiple determinants of demand, the demand curve can be interpreted as a reduced view of the demand function where only the price of the product is allowed to vary. Any other variables are assumed to remain at a fixed level. For the previous demand function for broadband service, suppose we assume A is fixed at \$5000, CP is fixed at \$25, and DIPC is fixed at \$33,000. If you substitute these values into the demand function and aggregate constant terms, the demand function becomes

$$Q = 64{,}000 - 800\,P.$$

Recall that demand curves are usually expressed with price as a function of quantity. With some basic algebra the equation of the demand curve can be written as

$$P = \$80 - \$0.00125\,Q.$$

What happens to the demand curve if one of the other variables is a different value? Well, in short, the demand curve would shift. Suppose the competitor decides to increase its price to \$35. Repeating the preceding steps, the demand function simplifies to

$$Q = 66{,}000 - 800\,P$$

or, expressed with P as a function of Q,

$$P = \$82.50 - 0.00125 \ Q.$$

Figure 3.1 shows a graph of the demand curve before and after the shift. Effectively, the result is that the broadband firm would see its demand increase by 2000 customers per month, or alternatively, the firm could raise its price to $32.50 and still maintain 40,000 customers per month.

Forecasting Demand

Identifying the key determinants of demand and developing demand functions gives a business manager a better understanding of his customers. A benefit of that understanding is an improved accuracy in forecasting the demand levels for their products and services in an upcoming period. Most businesses need to plan production activities well in advance of when the goods and services are actually provided to the consumer. Businesses need to have an adequately sized operation, have a sufficient staff

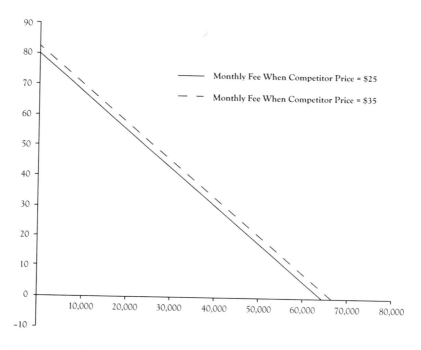

Figure 3.1. Shift in demand curve for broadband service caused by increase of competitor price from $25/month to $35/month.

in terms of size and training, and obtain any necessary resources for production. These capabilities are usually not possible to achieve overnight. For some goods, production is a process that takes significant time from initiation to completion, such as constructing apartments or office space that will be leased to customers. Even businesses that provide products or services "made to order," where most of the direct organization or production activities occur after a purchase is made, usually need to have supplies, trained labor, and management structures in place in advance of the order to be in a position to negotiate a sale.

Without some concrete estimate of what level of demand will result after these planning, designing, and production activities, a business may find itself with an excess of unused capacity or unable to serve the demand that follows. Excess capability is costly because idle resources have an opportunity cost but do not contribute to sales or revenue, especially when the unused resources spoil and cannot be used at a later time. When businesses set production targets too low, they discover missed opportunities for profit and unmet demand that is likely to discourage those consumers from being customers in the future.

To a limited extent, a business may be able to alter future demand to be more in line with its capacity because it has control over some determinants of demand, like pricing, promotion, and location. If the business is surprised by demand levels that are higher or lower than expected, these market strategy elements can be adjusted to either stimulate or diminish demand to conform to its production capabilities. Still, the financial performance of an enterprise is improved when the demand is consistent with the levels anticipated in the initial planning stages.

Further, most businesses are not in control of all the key determinants of demand. The business cannot control the direction of the overall economy and consumer incomes. The business may be able to guess at, but not control, actions by other companies that sell substitute and complementary goods and services. Anticipating the impact of these outside forces is critical.

Businesses can improve demand forecasting with their demand functions using the future values of determinant variables in those demand functions. Forecasts for widely followed economic indicators like disposable income are available from public releases or private forecasting services. If the business has a record of data for these uncontrollable variables, they can apply quantitative forecasting techniques like time series analysis or develop casual models that relate these factors to other variables that can be forecast. Readers are encouraged to look at a text in business forecasting for assistance in doing quantitative forecasts.[5]

For variables where past patterns may not continue into the future, like competitor actions on pricing and promotion or unexpected climate events, a business can construct scenarios in which management postulates settings for these factors and then develops a demand forecast for each scenario. Although the future will almost certainly not conform exactly to any single scenario, the exercise prepares them to monitor for changes in these factors and be ready to make a prompt response whenever a similar scenario emerges.

Elasticity of Demand

Another use of a mathematical demand function is measuring how sensitive demand is to changes in the level of one of the determinants. Suppose we would like to assess whether the demand for broadband service will change much in response to a change in its price. One indicator of the level of response to a price change is the coefficient of the price term in the demand function equation, $-800\ P$. The interpretation of the coefficient -800 is that for each increase of \$1 in the monthly subscriber price, the number of monthly subscribers will decrease by 800 subscribers.

This observation provides some insight, particularly if the broadband firm is considering a price change and would like to know the impact on the number of subscribers. However, for someone who measures price in terms of a different currency, say Japanese yen, a conversion to U.S. dollars would be needed to appreciate whether the demand change implied by the coefficient value is large or modest. Another limitation of this approach to measuring the responsiveness of demand to a determinant of demand is that the observation may not apply readily to other communities that may have a larger or smaller population of potential customers.

An alternative approach to measuring the sensitivity of demand to its determinant factors is to assess the ratio of percentage change in demand to the percentage change in its determinant factor. This type of measurement is called an *elasticity of demand*.

Assessing the elasticity of demand relative to changes in the price of the good or service being consumed is called the *own-price elasticity* or usually just the *price elasticity*. As an illustration of this, suppose we want to measure the sensitivity of demand for broadband services corresponding to a modest change in its price. First, to determine the price elasticity, you need to clearly understand the settings for all the determinant factors because elasticity changes if you look at a different configuration of factor levels. Suppose we decide to find the price elasticity when P = $30, A = $5000, CP = $25, and DIPC = $33,000. Earlier we determined that the demand quantity at this setting was Q = 40,000 monthly subscribers.

If we let the price increase by 10% from $30 to $33 and repeat the calculation of Q in the demand function, the value of Q will decline to 37,600 subscribers, which is a decline of 2400 customers. As a percentage of 40,000 monthly customers, this would be a 6% decrease. So the price elasticity here would be

$$\text{Price elasticity} = -6\%/10\% = -0.6.$$

Since the law of demand states that quantity demanded will drop when its price increases and quantity demanded will increase when its price decreases, price elasticities are usually negative numbers (other than special cases like Giffen goods, described earlier in this chapter).

Goods and services are categorized as being *price elastic* whenever the price elasticity is more negative than −1. In this category, the percentage change in quantity will be greater than the percentage change in price if you ignore the negative sign.

When the computed price elasticity is between 0 and −1, the good or service is considered to be *price inelastic*. This does not mean that demand does not respond to changes in price, but only that the response on a percentage basis is lower than the percentage change in price when the negative sign is ignored.

In those rare instances where price elasticities are positive, the product violates the law of demand. Again, these are similar to the Giffen goods discussed earlier.

By assessing sensitivity to changes on a percentage basis, it does not matter what units are used in the variable measurements. We could have constructed our demand function with a price measurement in cents or euros, and the price elasticity would have been the same. Also, if we wanted to compare the price elasticity of broadband service in this community with the price elasticity of broadband service in a larger community, we could compare the price elasticities directly without any need for further adjustment.

Another important class of elasticities is the response of demand to changes in income, or the *income elasticity*. For our broadband example, if we were to calculate the income elasticity at the same point where we calculated the price elasticity, we would have found an elasticity of 0.33. The interpretation of this value is as follows: For an increase of 1% in income levels, demand for broadband will increase by 0.33%.

When income elasticity of a product is greater than one, we call the product a *cyclic good*. The adjective "cyclic" suggests that this demand is sensitive to changes in the business cycle and will generally change more on a percentage basis than income levels. Luxury goods that customers can do without in hard economic times often fall in this category.

When income elasticity is between zero and one, we call the product a *noncyclic good*. Our broadband service falls in this category. The demand for noncyclic goods tends to move up and down with income levels, but not as strongly on a percentage basis. Most of the staple goods and services we need are noncyclic.

Normally we would expect demand for a good or service to increase when incomes increase and decrease when incomes decrease, other things being equal. However, there are arguably some exceptions that do not behave this way. Low-cost liquor, which might see increased use in hard economic times, is one of these possible exceptions. When income elasticity is negative, we call the product a *countercyclic good*.

When elasticities are calculated to measure the response of demand to price changes for a different good or service, say either a substitute product or complementary product, we call the calculated value a *cross-price elasticity*. Cross-price elasticities tend to be positive for substitute goods and negative for complementary goods. In our example, the competitor's service is a substitute good. If we calculate the cross-price elasticity for changes in the competitor's price on demand for broadband service at the point examined earlier, the result is 0.125.

Elasticities can be calculated for any factor on demand that can be expressed quantitatively. In our example, we could also calculate an advertising elasticity, which has a value of 0.5 at the given settings for the four factors in our demand function. This value indicates that an increase of 1% in our monthly advertising will result in a 0.5% increase in subscribers.

In interpreting and comparing elasticities, it is important to be clear whether the elasticity applies to a single business in a market or to all sellers in a market. Some elasticities, like price elasticities and advertising elasticities, tend to reflect greater sensitivity to changes in the factor when an elasticity is calculated for a single business than when assessed for the total demand for all sellers in a market. For example, we noted earlier that consumers will be unable to decrease gasoline consumption much, at least immediately, even if gasoline prices climb dramatically. This implies that gasoline is very price inelastic. However, this observation really applies to the gasoline industry as a whole. Suppose there was a street intersection in a city that has a gasoline station on every corner selling effectively the same product at about the same price, until one station increases its price dramatically (believing gasoline was highly inelastic to changes in price, so why not), but the other three stations leave their price where it was. If prices were clearly displayed, most customers would avoid the station that tried to increase the price and that station would see nearly all of its business disappear. In this situation where the competitors' goods are highly substitutable, the price elasticity for a single gasoline station would be very price elastic.

Consumption Decisions in the Short Run and the Long Run

The main reason most consumers are unable to respond very quickly to an increase in gasoline prices is because there is not an effective substitute for automobile travel. However, if consumers were convinced that gasoline prices were going to continue to rise into the foreseeable future, they would gradually make changes to their lifestyles so that they are able to reduce gasoline consumption significantly. They could purchase more fuel-efficient cars or cars that use an alternative fuel, or they could change jobs or change residences so that they are closer to their places of employment, shopping, and such.

Economists distinguish short-run decisions from long-run decisions. A consumer decision is considered *short run* when her consumption will occur soon enough to be constrained by existing household assets, personal commitments, and know-how. Given sufficient time to remove these constraints, the consumer can change her consumption patterns and make additional improvements in the utility of consumption. Decisions affecting consumption far enough into the future so that any such adjustments can be made are called *long-run* decisions.

Demand functions and demand curves can be developed for short-run or long-run time horizons. Short-run demand curves are easier to develop because they estimate demand in the near future and generally do not require a long history of data on consumption and its determinant factors. Because long-run demand must account for changes in consumption styles, it requires longer histories of data and greater sophistication.

Elasticities of demand in the short run can differ substantially from elasticities in the long run. Long-run price elasticities for a product are generally of higher magnitude than their short-run counterparts because the consumer has sufficient time to change consumption styles.

There is so much uncertainty about long-run consumption that these analyses are usually limited to academic and government research. Short-run analyses, on the other hand, are feasible for many analysts working for the businesses that must estimate demand in order to make production decisions.

Price Discrimination

In the ice cream bar summer business in chapter 2, we presumed that the student operators would decide on a price to charge. All ice cream bars would be sold at that price. We reasoned that more ice cream bars could be sold as the price is decreased. If the students decide to charge $1.50 per ice cream bar, a potential customer will decide if the utility of the ice cream bar is sufficiently high for them to be willing to give up $1.50 of their wealth. If not, they will walk away without making a purchase. If the students instead decide to charge $1.80 per ice cream bar, the demand curve indicated that 6000 fewer unit purchases would occur, meaning 6000 of those purchases were not worth $1.80 to the purchasers. However, some of the customers would have been willing to pay over $2.00, and fewer even more than $2.50 or $3.00.

When all consumers pay the same price, some of them get a kind of surplus because they would have been willing to pay more for the ice cream bar. Sellers may wish they were able to charge customers the maximum amount they are willing to pay, which would result in more revenue and no added cost. In economics, the term for charging different prices to different customers is called *price discrimination*. Economists have actually defined multiple types of price discrimination, called first-degree price discrimination, second-degree price discrimination, and third-degree price discrimination.

First-degree price discrimination is an attempt by the seller to leave the price unannounced in advance and charge each customer the highest price they would be willing to pay for the purchase. If perfectly executed, this would meet the ideal of getting the greatest revenue possible from sales. Unfortunately, anything close to perfect execution of first-degree price discrimination is unrealistic because customers have an incentive to not reveal how much they would be willing to pay and instead try to pay as little as possible. Attempts to sell using first-degree price discrimination may be illegal as well, as it may be deemed discriminatory in the legal sense of the word.

Some commercial dealings resemble attempts at first-degree price discrimination. Sometimes there is no set price, and the buyer and seller negotiate a price. This is the customary way that automobiles have been sold in the United States. The process may start with a preannounced price, but one that is usually higher than the seller actually expects to receive. This falls short of pure first-degree discrimination because the buyer is probably able to negotiate down from the most he would pay, possibly quite a bit if the buyer is a good negotiator. In addition, there is time and effort expended in the negotiating, which is a kind of cost to the transaction that the buyer may see as part of the purchase cost and the seller may see as an added cost of business.

Goods and services are sometimes sold or purchased via an auction. This is usually an effective means when the seller has a limited number of items to sell. Run properly, an auction will distinguish those willing to pay more, although it probably will not manage to get a bid as high as the maximum the buyer would have paid. Again, the cost of operating an auction is expensive in comparison to selling using a set, preannounced price.

Businesses that sell a product that is in demand with no good substitute available will sometimes employ a sliding price, where they begin selling at a very high price that is attractive to relatively few consumers.

After a time when presumably those high-value customers make their purchases, the business will drop the price somewhat and attract purchases from another group that was willing pay slightly less than the first group. Successive price drops can continue until it would be unprofitable for the seller to drop the price any lower. Sliding prices are sometimes used with products that employ new technologies, when the initial seller has the market to itself, at least for a while, and offers a got-to-have item for some customers. Of course, although these eager customers may be willing to pay more, they may be aware of this pricing strategy and delay their purchase, so this approach will not extract the full value customers would have been willing to pay.

When goods and services are sold according to a preannounced price, the customary arrangement is that the charge for multiple items is the price times the number of items. This is called *linear pricing*. However, customers differ in the volume they are interested in purchasing. A business may benefit by offering different prices to those who purchase in larger volumes because either they can increase their profit with the increased volume sales or their costs per unit decrease when items are purchased in volume. Businesses can create alternative pricing methods that distinguish high-volume buyers from low-volume buyers. This is *second-degree price discrimination.*

A donut shop might offer a free donut to anyone who purchases a whole dozen because the purchase requires less clerk time per donut sold and increases how many donuts get purchased. However, since only those who buy at least a dozen donuts get a free donut, the discount is limited to those people and not the customer who purchases just a donut or two. This would be second-degree price discrimination.

Another nonlinear pricing scheme to employ second-degree discrimination is a two-part price. A customer pays a flat charge to be a customer and then pays a per unit charge based on how much they consume. Some services like telephone service are primarily fixed cost and have a very small per unit variable cost. By charging telephone customers a flat monthly fee and low per unit charge, they encourage more use of the service than if they simply charged a linear price per unit and see more revenue in relation to costs. Membership stores that require customers to pay an entry fee before being allowed to shop, but offer lower prices than regular stores for purchased items, is another example of a two-part pricing.

Third-degree price discrimination is differential pricing to different groups of customers. One justification for this practice is that producing goods and services for sale to one identifiable group of customers is less than the cost of sales to another group of customers. For example, a publisher of music or books may be able to sell a music album or a book in electronic form for less cost than a physical form like a compact disc or printed text.

A second justification for charging different prices to different groups of customers is that one group may be more sensitive to price than the other group. Earlier we discussed elasticity of demand. If we separated the demand for the two groups into separate demand curves, at any given price the more price sensitive group will have stronger negative price elasticity. Sellers are able to increase economic profit by charging a lower price to the price-elastic group and a higher price to the more price-inelastic group. As an example, 25 years ago music was sold in two formats: cassette tapes and compact discs. The production cost of a cassette tape was roughly equivalent to a compact disc, but music on compact discs often retailed at a higher price because it was perceived that customers of compact discs were more demanding of quality and more price inelastic.

To apply third-degree price discrimination, the seller must be able to clearly identify and sort the customer by a salient characteristic. For example, a cable provider may be aware that existing subscribers are price inelastic relative to other households that are not existing customers. The cable provider will typically charge reduced rates to attract new customers and is able to execute the price discrimination because it knows whether a customer is an existing customer or not. A sports clothing retailer may know that fans of a team are more price inelastic in the purchase of apparel displaying the name or mascot of that team than customers who are not fans. However, if the clothing retailer were to attempt to charge differential prices, the customers who are fans would have the incentive to disguise that characteristic, so third-degree price discrimination would not work well in this case.

CHAPTER 4

Cost and Production

In the previous two chapters we examined the economics underlying decisions related to which goods and services a business concern will sell, where it will sell them, how it will sell them, and in what quantities. Another challenge for management is to determine how to acquire and organize its production resources to best support those commitments. In this chapter and in the following chapter we will be discussing key concepts and principles from microeconomics that guide its organization and production activities to improve profitability and be able to compete effectively.

A number of highly useful methodologies have been developed based on the concepts and principles discussed. This text will not address specific techniques for tracking costs and planning production activities. Readers seeking guidance on these tasks might consult a text on cost accounting or operations management.[1]

Average Cost Curves

In chapter 2, we cited average cost as a key performance measure in producing a good or service. Average cost reflects the cost on a per unit basis. A portion of the average cost is the amount of variable costs that can be assigned to the production unit. The other portion is the allocation of fixed costs (specifically those fixed costs that are not sunk), apportioned to each production unit.

The average cost generally varies as a function of the production volume per period. Since fixed costs do not increase with quantity produced, at least in the short run where production capabilities are relatively set, the portion of the average cost attributable to fixed cost is very high for small production volume but declines rapidly and then levels off as the volume increases.

The portion of average cost related to the variable cost usually changes less dramatically in response to production volume than the average fixed cost. In fact, in the example of the ice cream bar business in chapter 2, we assumed the average variable cost of an ice cream bar would remain $0.30 per unit whether the operation sold a small volume or large volume of ice cream bars. However, in actual production environments, average variable cost may fluctuate with volume.

At very low production volumes, resources may not be used efficiently, so the variable cost per unit is higher. For example, suppose the ice cream bar venture operators purchase those bars wholesale from a vendor who delivers them in a truck with a freezer. Since the vendor's charge for ice cream bars must cover the cost of the truck driver and truck operation, a large delivery that fills the truck is likely to cost less per ice cream bar than a very small delivery.

At the same time, pushing production levels to the upper limits of an operation's capability can result in other inefficiencies and cause the average variable cost to increase. For example, in order to increase production volume in a factory, it may be necessary to pay workers to work overtime at a rate 1.5 times their normal pay rate. Another example is that machines may be overworked to drive higher volume but result in either less efficiency or higher maintenance cost, which translates into an increase in average variable cost.

Figure 4.1 shows a general breakdown of average cost into average fixed cost and average variable cost. The figure reflects the earlier situations of variable cost inefficiencies at very low and very high production volumes. Note that even with the continued decline in the average fixed cost, there is a production level (marked Q^*) where the average total cost is at its lowest value. Economists called the production volume where average cost is at the lowest value the *capacity* of the operation.

In conversational language, we often think of capacity of a container as the maximum volume the container can hold. In that sense of the word, it seems awkward to call the production level Q^* the capacity when the graph indicates that it is possible to produce at higher volume levels but just that the average cost per unit will be higher. However, even in physics, the volume in a container can be changed by the use of pressure or temperature, so volume is not limited by the capacity under normal pressures and temperatures.

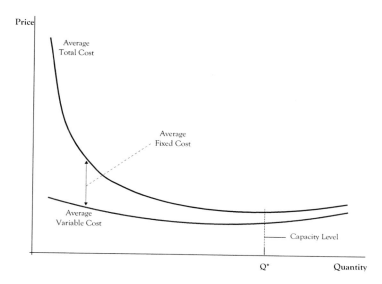

Figure 4.1. Breakdown of average cost function into variable cost and fixed cost component. The production level corresponding to the lowest point on the graph for average cost indicates the short-run capacity of the business operation.

In the economic sense of the word, we might think of capacity as the volume level where we have the most efficient operation in terms of average cost. Many businesses can operate over capacity, up to some effective physical limit, but in so doing will pay for that supplemental production volume in higher costs, due to needing to employ either more expensive resources or less productive resources, creating congestion that slows production, or overusing resources that results in higher maintenance costs per unit.

If the price earned by the business at these overcapacity volumes is sufficiently high, the firm may realize more profit by operating over capacity than at the capacity point where total average cost is at its lowest. Similarly, if demand is weak and customers will pay a price well in excess of average cost only at volumes lower than capacity, the firm will probably do better by operating below capacity. However, if a firm that is operating well above capacity or well below capacity does not see this as a temporary situation, the discrepancy suggests that the firm is sized either too small or too large. The firm may be able to improve profits in future production periods by resizing its operations, which will readjust the capacity point. If the firm operates in a very competitive market, there may even be little potential for profit for firms that are not operating near their capacity level.

Long-Run Average Cost and Scale

In the last chapter, we distinguished short-run demand from long-run demand to reflect the range of options for consumers. In the short run, consumers were limited in their choices by their current circumstances of lifestyles, consumption technologies, and understanding. A long-run time frame was of sufficient length that the consumer had the ability to alter her lifestyle and technology and to improve her understanding, so as to result in improved utility of consumption.

There is a similar dichotomy of short-run production decisions and long-run production decisions for businesses. In the short run, businesses are somewhat limited by their facilities, skill sets, and technology. In the long run, businesses have sufficient time to expand, contract, or modify facilities. Businesses can add employees, reduce employees, or retrain or redeploy employees. They can change technology and the equipment used to carry out their businesses.

The classification of short-run planning is more an indication of some temporary constraint on redefining the structure of a firm rather than a period of a specific length. In fact, there are varying degrees of short run. In a very brief period, say the coming week or month, there may be very little that most businesses can do. It will take at least that long to make changes in employees and they probably have contractual obligations to satisfy. Six months may be long enough to change employment structures and what supplies a firm uses, but the company is probably still limited to the facilities and technology they are using.

How long a period is needed until decisions are long term varies by the kind of organization or industry. A retail outlet might easily totally redefine itself in a matter of months, so for them any decisions going out a year or longer are effectively long-term decisions. For electricity power generators, it can take 20 years to plan, get approvals, and construct a new power generation facility, and their long-term period can be in terms of decades.

One important characteristic that distinguishes short-run production decisions and long-run production decisions is in the nature of costs. In the short run, there are fixed costs and variable costs. However, in the long run, since the firm has the flexibility to change anything about its operations (within the scope of what is technologically possible and they can afford), all costs in long-run production decisions can be regarded as variable costs.

Another important distinction between short-run production and long-run production is in the firm's ability to alter its capacity. In a decidedly short-run time frame, the firm's capacity or point of lowest average cost is effectively fixed. The firm may elect to operate either under or slightly over their capacity depending on the strength of market demand but cannot readily optimize production for that selected output level. In the long run, the firm is able to make decisions that alter its capacity point by resizing operations to where the firm expects to have the best stream of profits over time.

Because a business has the ability to redesign all of its operations to suit a targeted level of production, average cost curves for long-run planning are flatter than short-run average cost curves. If it appears that a low-volume operation would yield the best returns, the firm can be downsized to remove the cost of excess capacity and arrive at a lower average cost than would be achievable in the short run. By expanding its capacity, a firm would be able to perhaps even lower average cost, but certainly avoid the inefficiencies of being overcapacity, should higher production levels appear to be better.

One way to think of a long-run average cost curve is that each point on the curve reflects the lowest possible average cost of an operation resized to be optimal for that level of production. For example, in Figure 4.2, the long-run average cost on curve LRAC at a production rate of 1000 units per period is the lowest cost, or cost at the capacity point, for a cost structure reflected by short-run average cost curve $SRAC_1$. The long-run average cost at a production rate of 2000 units per production period is the lowest cost for average cost curve $SRAC_2$ (which has a capacity of 2000). The long-run average cost at a production rate of 3000 units per production would be the average cost at capacity for $SRAC_3$.

Like short-run average cost curves, long-run average cost curves trend downward at low target production rates, although the rate of decline

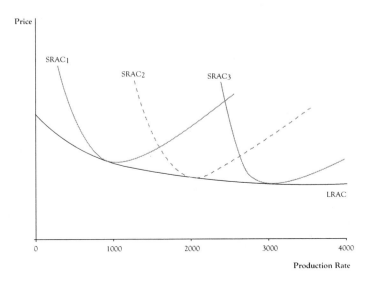

Figure 4.2. Graph of long-run average cost (LRAC) function shown as the short-run average cost (SRAC) at capacity for different scales of operation.

in the long-run average cost curve is somewhat flatter due to the ability to readjust all factors of production. The typical reason for this declining long-run average cost curve at low production levels is because there are efficiencies in cost or production that can be exploited for modest increases in quantity. For example, for a business that is manufacturing major appliances or vehicles that require several assembly steps, in a larger operation it is possible to assign different assembly steps to different workers and, via this specialization, speed up the rate of production over what would be possible if the firm hired the same workers with each worker performing all assembly steps. As we pointed out in the previous chapter, customers who buy in large quantities can sometimes buy at a lower per unit price. Since most firms are buyers as well as sellers, and larger firms will buy in larger quantities, they can reduce the contribution of acquired parts and materials to the average cost.

The ability to reduce long-run average cost due to increased efficiencies in production and cost will usually eventually subside. The production level at which the long-run average cost curve flattens out is called the *minimum efficient scale.* (Since the business is able to adjust all factors of production in the long run, it can effectively rescale the entire operation, so the target production level is sometimes called the *scale* of the business.) In competitive seller markets, the ability of a firm to achieve minimum efficient scale is crucial to its survival. If one firm is producing at minimum efficient scale and another firm is operating below minimum efficient scale, it is possible for the larger firm to push market prices below the cost of the smaller firm, while continuing to charge a price that exceeds its average cost. Facing the prospect of sustained losses, the smaller firm usually faces a choice between getting larger or dropping out of the market.

The increase in capacity needed to achieve minimum efficient scale varies by the type of business. A bicycle repair shop might achieve minimum efficient scale with a staff of four or five employees and be able to operate at an average cost that is no different than a shop of 40 to 50 repair persons. At the other extreme, electricity distribution services and telephone services that have very large fixed asset costs and low variable costs may see the long-run average cost curve decline even for large production levels and therefore would have a very high minimum efficient scale.

Most firms have a long-run average cost curve that declines and then flattens out; however, in some markets the long-run average cost may actually rise after some point. This phenomenon often indicates a limitation in some factors of production or a decline in quality in factors of production if the scale increases enough. For example, in agriculture some land is clearly better suited to certain crops than other land. In order to match the yield of the best acreage on land of lower quality, it may be necessary to spend more on fertilizer, water, or pest control, thereby increasing the average cost of production for all acreage used.

Businesses that are able to lower their average costs by increasing the scale of their operation are said to have *economies of scale*. Firms that will see their average costs increase if they further increase their scale will experience *diseconomies of scale*. Businesses that have achieved at least their minimum efficient scale and would see the long-run average cost remain about the same with continued increases in scale may be described as having *constant economies of scale*.

The impact of an increase of scale on production is sometimes interpreted in terms of "returns to scale." The assessment of returns to scale is based on the response to the following question: If all factors of production (raw materials, labor, energy, equipment time, etc.) where increased by a set percentage (say all increased by 10%), would the percent increase in potential quantity of output created be greater, the same, or less than the percent increase in all factors of production? If potential output increases by a higher percent, operations are said to have increasing returns to scale. If output increases by the same percent, the operations show constant returns to scale. If the percent growth in outputs is less than the percent increase in inputs used, there are decreasing returns to scale.

Returns to scale are related to the concept of economies of scale, yet there is a subtle difference. The earlier example of gained productivity of labor specialization when the labor force is increased would contribute to increasing returns to scale. Often when there are increasing returns to scale there are economies of scale because the higher rate of growth in output translates to decrease in average cost per unit. However, economies of scale may occur even if there were constant returns to scale, such as if there were volume discounts for buying supplies in larger quantities. Economies of scale mean average cost decreases as the scale increases, whereas increasing returns to scale are restricted to the physical ratio between the increase in units of output relative to proportional increase in the number of inputs used.

Likewise, decreasing returns to scale often translate to diseconomies of scale. If increasing the acreage used for a particular crop by using less productive acreage results in a smaller increase in yield than increase in acreage, there are decreasing returns to scale. Unless the acreage costs less to use, there will be an increase in average cost per unit of crop output, indicating diseconomies of scale.

Economies of Scope and Joint Products

Most businesses provide multiple goods and services; in some cases, the number of goods and services is quite large. Whereas the motivation for providing multiple products may be driven by consumer expectations, a common attraction is the opportunity to reduce per unit costs. When a venture can appreciate such cost savings, the opportunity is called an *economy of scope.*

Of course, not just any aggregation of goods and services will create economies of scope. For significant economies of scope, the goods and services need to be similar in nature or utilize similar raw materials, facilities, production processes, or knowledge.

One type of cost savings is the ability to share fixed costs across the product and service lines so that the total fixed costs are less than if the operations were organized separately. For example, suppose we have a company that expands from selling one product to two similar products. The administrative functions for procurement, receiving, accounts payable, inventory management, shipping, and accounts receivable in place for the first product can usually support the second product with just a modest increase in cost.

A second type of cost savings occurs from doing similar activities in larger volume and reducing per unit variable costs. If multiple goods and services require the same raw materials, the firm may be able to acquire the raw materials at a smaller per unit cost by purchasing in larger volume. Similarly, labor that is directly related to variable cost may not need to be increased proportionally for additional products due to the opportunity to exploit specialization or better use of idle time.

In some cases, two or more products may be natural by-products of a production process. For example, in refining crude oil to produce gasoline to fuel cars and trucks, the refining process will create lubricants, fertilizers, petrochemicals, and other kinds of fuels. Since the refining process requires heat, the excess heat can be used to create steam for electricity generation that more than meets the refinery's needs and may be sold to an electric utility. When multiple products occur at the result of a combined process, they are called *joint products* and create a natural opportunity for an economy of scope.

As with economies of scale, the opportunities for economies of scope generally dissipate after exploiting the obvious combinations of goods and services. At some point, the complexity of trying to administer a firm with too many goods and services will offset any cost savings, particularly if the goods and services share little in terms of production resources or processes. However, sometimes firms discover scope economies that are not so obvious and can realize increased economic profits, at least for a time until the competition copies their discovery.

Cost Approach Versus Resource Approach to Production Planning

The conventional approach to planning production is to start with the goods and services that a firm intends to provide and then decide what production configuration will achieve the intended output at the lowest cost. This is the *cost approach* to production planning.[2] Once output goals are set, the expected revenue is essentially determined, so any remaining opportunity for profit requires reducing the cost as much as possible.

Although this principle of cost minimization is simple, actually achieving true minimization in practice is not feasible for most ventures of any complexity. Rather, minimization of costs is a target that is not fully realized because the range of production options is wide and the actual resulting costs may differ from what was expected in the planning phase.

Additionally, as we saw in chapter 2, the decision about whether to provide a good or service and how much to provide requires an assessment of marginal cost. Due to scale effects, this marginal cost may vary with the output level, so firms may face a circular problem of needing to know the marginal cost to decide on the outputs, but the marginal cost may change depending on the output level selected. This dilemma may be addressed by iteration between output planning and production/procurement planning until there is consistency. Another option is to use sophisticated computer models that determine the optimal output levels and minimum cost production configurations simultaneously.

Among the range of procurement and production activities that a business conducts to create its goods and services, the firm may be more proficient or expert in some of the activities, at least relative to its competition. For example, a firm may be world class in factory production but only about average in the cost effectiveness of its marketing activities. In situations where a firm excels in some components of its operations, there may be an opportunity for improved profitability by recognizing these key areas, sometimes called *core competencies* in the business strategy literature, and then determining what kinds of goods or services would best exploit these capabilities. This is the *resource approach* to the planning of production.[3]

Conceptually, either planning approach will lead to similar decisions about what goods and services to provide and how to arrange production to do that. However, given the wide ranges of possible outputs and organizations of production to provide them, firms are not likely to attain truly optimal organization, particularly after the fact. The cost approach is often easier to conduct, particularly for a firm that is already in a particular line of business and can make incremental improvements to reduce cost. However, in solving the problem of how to create the goods and services at minimal cost, there is some risk of myopic focus that dismisses opportunities to make the best use of core competencies. The resource approach encourages more out-of-the-box thinking that may lead a business toward a major restructuring.

Marginal Revenue Product and Derived Demand

In chapter 2, we discussed the principle for profit maximization stating that, absent constraints on production, the optimal output levels for the goods and services occur when marginal revenue equals marginal cost. This principle can be applied in determining the optimal level of any production resource input using the concepts of marginal product and marginal revenue product.

The *marginal product* of a production input is the amount of additional output that would be created if one more unit of the input were obtained and processed. For example, if an accounting firm sells accountant time as a service and each hired accountant is typically billed to clients 1500 hours per year, this quantity would be the marginal product of hiring an additional accountant.

The *marginal revenue product* of a production input is the marginal revenue created from the marginal product resulting from one additional unit of the input. The marginal revenue product would be the result of multiplying the marginal product of the input times the marginal revenue of the output. For the example in the previous paragraph, suppose that at the current output levels, the marginal revenue from an additional billed hour of accountant service is $100. The marginal revenue product of an additional accountant would be 1500 times $100, or $150,000.

In determining if a firm is using the optimal level on an input, the marginal revenue product for an additional unit of input can be compared to the marginal cost of a unit of the input. If the marginal revenue product exceeds the marginal input cost, the firm can improve profitability by increasing the use of that input and the resulting increase in output. If the marginal cost of the input exceeds the marginal revenue product, profit will improve by decreasing the use of that input and the corresponding decrease in output. At the optimal level, the marginal revenue product and marginal cost of the input would be equal.

Suppose the marginal cost to hire an additional accountant in the previous example was $120,000. The firm would improve its profit by $30,000 by hiring one more accountant.

As noted earlier in the discussion of marginal revenue, the marginal revenue will change as output is increased, usually declining as output levels increase. Correspondingly, the marginal revenue product will generally decrease as the input and corresponding output continue to be increased. This phenomenon is called the *law of diminishing marginal returns to an input.* So, for the accounting firm, although they may realize an additional $30,000 in profit by hiring one more accountant, that does not imply they would realize $3,000,000 more in profits by hiring 100 more accountants.

If the marginal revenue product is measured at several possible input levels and graphed, the pattern suggests a relationship between quantity of input and marginal revenue product, as shown in Figure 4.3. Due to

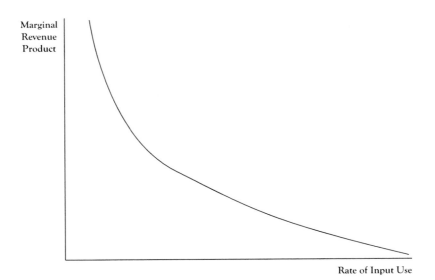

Figure 4.3. Typical pattern of a derived demand curve relating the marginal revenue product to quantity of input employed in production.

the law of diminishing marginal returns, this relationship will generally be negative. Thus the relationship looks much like the demand curve corresponding to output levels. In fact, this relationship is a transformation of the firm's demand curve, expressed in terms of the equivalent marginal revenue product relative to number of units of input used. Due to the connection to the demand curve for output, the relationship depicted in Figure 4.3 is called a *derived demand curve*.

One difficulty in comparing marginal revenue product to the marginal cost of an input is that the mere increase in any single input is usually not enough in itself to create more units of output. For example, simply acquiring more bicycle frames will not result in the ability to make more bicycles, unless the manufacturer acquires more wheels, tires, brakes, seats, and such to turn those frames into bicycles. In cases like this, sometimes the principle needs to be applied to a fixed mix of inputs rather than a single input.

For the accounting firm in the earlier example, the cost to acquire an additional accountant is not merely the salary he is paid. The firm will pay for benefits like retirement contribution and health care for the new employee. Further, additional inputs in the form of an office, computer, secretarial support, and such will be incurred. So the fact that the marginal revenue product of an accountant is $150,000 does not mean that the firm would benefit if the accountant were hired at any salary less than $150,000. Rather, it would profit if the additional cost of salary, benefits, office expense, secretarial support, and so on is less than $150,000.

Marginal Cost of Inputs and Economic Rent

In cases where inputs are in high supply at the current market price and the market for inputs is competitive, the marginal cost of an input is roughly equal to the actual cost of acquiring it. So, in such a situation, the principle described earlier can be expressed in terms of comparing the marginal revenue product to price to acquire the input(s). If the number of accountants seeking a job were fairly substantial and competitive, the actual per unit costs involved in hiring one more accountant would be the marginal cost.

If the market of inputs is less competitive, a firm may have to pay a little higher than the prevailing market price to acquire more units because they will need to be hired away from another firm. In this situation, the marginal cost of inputs may be higher than the price to acquire an additional unit because the resulting price increase for the additional unit may carry over to a price increase of all units being purchased.

Suppose the salary required to hire a new accountant will be higher than what the firm is currently paying accountants with the same ability. Once the firm pays a higher salary to get a new accountant, they may need to raise the salaries of the other similar accountants they already hired just to retain them. In this instance, the marginal cost of hiring one more accountant could be substantially more than the cost directly associated with adding the new accountant. As a result of the impact on other salaries and associated costs of the hire, the firm may decide that the highest salary for a new accountant that the firm can justify may be on the order of $50,000, even though the resulting marginal revenue product is substantially greater.

If inputs are available in a ready supply, or there are close substitutes available that are in ready supply, the price of an additional unit of input typically reflects either the opportunity cost related to the value of the next best use of that input or the minimum amount needed to induce a new unit to become available. However, there are some production inputs that may be in such limited supply that even further price increases will not attract new units to become available, at least not quickly. In these cases, the marginal revenue product for an input may still considerably exceed its marginal cost, even after all available inputs are in use. The sellers of these goods and services may be aware of this imbalance and insist on a price increase for the input up to a level that brings marginal cost in balance with marginal revenue product. The difference between the amount the provider of the limited input supply is able to charge and the minimum amount that would have been necessary to induce the provider to sell the unit to the firm is called *economic rent.*

Suppose a contracting firm was hired to do emergency repairs to a major bridge. Due to the time deadline, the firm will need to hire additional construction workers who are already in the area. Normally, these workers may have been willing to work for $70 per hour. However, sensing the contracting firm is being paid a premium for the repairs, meaning the marginal revenue product of labor is high, and there are a limited number of qualified workers available, the workers can insist on being paid as much as $200 per hour for the work. The difference of $130 would be economic rent caused by the shortage of qualified workers available on short notice.

Economic rent can occur in agriculture when highly productive land is in limited supply or in some labor markets like professional sports or commercial entertainment where there is a limited supply of people who have the skills or name recognition needed to make the activity successful.

Productivity and the Learning Curve

The resource view of production management is to make sure that all resources employed in the creation of goods and services are used as effectively as possible. Smart businesses assess the productivity of key production resources as a means of tracking improvements and in comparing their operations to those of other firms.

Earlier in this chapter we introduced the concept of marginal product. This measure reflects how productive an additional unit of that input would be in creating additional output. However, for some inputs, there are differences in marginal productivity across units. For example, in agriculture an acre of land in one location may be capable of better yields than an acre in another location. At any given input price, firms will seek to employ those units with the highest marginal product first.

In looking at the collective performance of a production operation, we need a measure of productivity that applies to all inputs being used rather than the last unit acquired. One means of doing this is using the measure of *average productivity*, which is a ratio of the total number of units of output divided by the total units of an input. An alternative measure of average productivity would be the total dollars in revenue or profit divided by the total units of an input.

Computations of average productivity make sense for key inputs around which production processes are designed. In the example of the accounting firm used in this chapter, the number of accountants is probably a good choice. Average productivity could be in the form of labor hours billed divided by accountants hired. If a firm managed to sell 1600 billable hours in 1 year, but only 1500 billable hours in another year, the earlier year indicated higher productivity.

In retail stores, a key resource is the amount of floor space. The productivity of a store could be measured by the total revenue over a period divided by the available square footage. This measure could be compared to the same measure for other stores in the retail chain or with similar competitor stores. Even sections within the store can be compared for which types of goods and services sold are most effective in generating sales, although given that costs vary too, a better productivity measure here may be profit contribution (revenue minus variable cost) per square foot.

The productivity of firms may change over time. In the case of labor, the productivity of individual workers will rise as they gain experience and new workers can be trained more effectively. There is also an improvement in overall productivity from the increased knowledge of management in how to employ productive resources better. These productivity gains from experience and improved knowledge are sometimes called *learning by doing*.[4]

In addition to the increased profit potential of improved productivity, new firms or firms starting new operations need to anticipate these gains in deciding whether to engage in a new venture. Often a venture will not look attractive if the assumed costs of production are based on the costs that apply in the initial periods of production. Learning improvements need to be considered as well. In some sense, decreased profits and even losses in the initial production periods are necessary investments for a successful long-term operation.

Improvements due to productivity gains will usually result in decreased average costs. The relationship between cumulative production experience and average cost is called the *learning curve*. An example appears in Figure 4.4. One point to be emphasized is that the quantity on the horizontal axis is *cumulative* production, or total production to date, rather than production rate per production period. This is *not* a scale effect *per se*. Even if the firm continues to produce at the same rate each period, it will see declines in the average cost per unit of output, especially in the initial stages of operation.

One numerical measure of the impact of learning on average cost is called the *doubling rate of reduction*. The doubling rate is the reduction in average cost that occurs each time *cumulative* production doubles. If the average cost declines by 15% each time cumulative production doubles, that would be its doubling rate. A learning curve with a doubling rate of

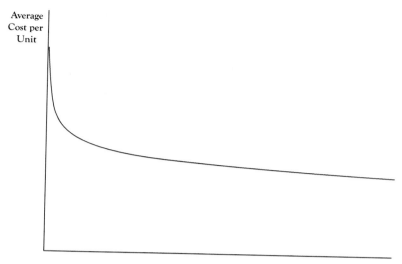

Figure 4.4. Pattern of a learning curve showing average cost declining by a fixed percentage for each doubling of cumulative output.

15% may be called an 85% learning curve to indicate the magnitude of the average cost compared to when cumulative production was only half as large.

Note that the number of units required to double cumulative production will get progressively higher. For example, if cumulative production now is 1000 units, the next doubling will occur at 2000 cumulative units, with the next doubling at 4000 cumulative units, and the following at 8000 cumulative units. Thus the rate of decline in average cost for each successive unit of production will diminish as cumulative production increases.

CHAPTER 5

Economics of Organization

For many years, the field of microeconomics focused primarily on the relationship between firms and the outside environment of consumers, suppliers, competitors, and regulators. Internally, it was assumed that a firm was able to measure the costs associated with any pattern of exchanges with the outside environment in order to determine the best production and marketing decisions. However, the conduct of the actual processes involved in production was not regarded as an issue of economics in itself. Rather, these matters were treated as issues of organizational behavior and organizational design to best assign, coordinate, and motivate employees, much like a military unit.

In recent decades, economists have applied and developed economic principles that inform a better understanding of activity inside the firm. One focus in this newer endeavor is the firm's decisions on which goods and services they will provide. A related topic of interest to economists is how much of the production activity will be done by the firm and how much will be purchased from other firms or contracted out to other businesses.

When a business elects to provide a large number of goods and services or has complex, multistage production operations, operations must be assigned to departments or divisions and the firm faces challenges in coordinating these units. Although organizational psychologists have addressed these issues for many years, economics has been able to provide some new insights.

Another issue in the design of a firm is motivation of units and individuals. In analyses based on organizational behavior, individuals are regarded as having psychological needs and the challenge to the organization is how to design procedures to meet those needs so that employees better support the needs of the organization. The new perspective from economics views an employee as an independent agent whose primary

objective is to maximize his own welfare and the challenge to the organization is to structure incentives in a manner that aligns the economic
interests of the firm with economic interests of the employee.

Reasons to Expand an Enterprise

Businesses usually sell multiple products or services, and they alter the
collection of goods and services provided over time. Several factors motivate changes in this composition and can result in decisions either to
expand an enterprise by increasing the range of goods and services offered
or to contract the enterprise by suspending production and sale of some
goods and services. In this section, we will list some key motivations
for expanding the range of an enterprise. Bear in mind that when these
motivations are absent or reversed, the same considerations can lead to
decisions to contract the range of the enterprise.

1. Earlier, in chapter 4, we discussed the concepts of economies of
   scale (cost per unit decreases as volume increases) and economies of
   scope (costs per unit of different goods can be reduced by producing
   multiple products using the same production resources). Businesses
   often expand to exploit these economies.
2. As we will see in chapter 7, in markets with few sellers that each
   provide a large fraction of the goods or services available, the sellers possess an advantage over buyers in commanding higher prices.
   Businesses will often either buy out competitors or increase production with the intent to drive competitors out of the seller market in
   order to gain market power.
3. Many businesses sell products that are intermediate, rather than
   final, goods. Their customers are other businesses that take the
   goods or services they purchase and combine or enhance them to
   provide other goods and services. As a result, the profit that is earned
   in the production of a final product will be distributed across several
   firms that contributed to the creation of that good. However, the
   profit may not be evenly distributed across the contributing firms
   or proportional to their costs. Sometimes a firm will recognize the
   higher profit potential of the firms that supply them or the firms to

which they are suppliers and will decide to participate in those more lucrative production stages.

4. Due to the considerable uncertainties of future costs, revenues, and profits and the need for firms to commit resources before these uncertainties are resolved, business is a risky prospect. Just as investors can mitigate the inherent risk of owning stocks by purchasing shares in different firms across somewhat unrelated industries, large firms can reduce some of their risk by producing unrelated products or services. Additionally, there may be increased efficiencies in movement of resources between different production operations when done by the same company.

Classifying Business Expansion in Terms of Value Chains

We noted earlier that many businesses sell goods or services that are intended to help other businesses in the creation of their goods and services. Many of the goods we consume as individuals are the result of a sequence of production operations that may involve several firms. If the final goods are traced backward through the intermediate goods that were acquired and utilized, we can usually envision the participant firms in a creation process as a network of production activities or a sequence of production stages.

For example, consider a loaf of bread purchased at a grocery store. The grocery store may purchase the loaf from a distributor of bakery products. The distributor likely purchased the loaf from a baking company. In order to produce the loaf of bread, the bakery would need flour and yeast, along with packaging material. These may be purchased from other businesses. The flour came from a grain grinding process that may have been done by a different business. The business that ground the grain would need grain that may have come from an agricultural cooperative, which in turn was the recipient of the grain from a farmer. In order to grow and harvest the grain, the farmer needs seed, tractors, and fuel, which are usually obtained from other sources.

Each of the firms or production operations that contributes to the creation of the final product can be considered as adding value to the resources they acquire in their completion of a stage of the creation process. Since the network of operations that account for the creation of a product can often be represented by a sequence of stages, the network is commonly called the *value chain* for the product.

Figure 5.1 shows a generic value chain for a manufactured good. This value chain begins with the raw materials that eventually go into the product that must be acquired, possibly by mining (e.g., metal) or harvesting (e.g., wood). Next, the raw material is processed into a material that can be used to create parts in the next stage. Using these parts, the next stage of the value chain is the assembly of the product. Once assembled, the product must be distributed to the point of sale. In the final stage, a retailer sells the finished product to the consumer.

Business expansions are classified based on the relationship of the newly integrated activity to prior activities engaged in by the firm. If the new activity is in the same stage of that value chain or a similar value chain, the expansion is called *horizontal integration*. If the new activity is in the same value chain but at a different stage, the expansion is called *vertical integration*. If the new activity is part of a quite different value chain, the new combined entity would be called a *conglomerate merger*.

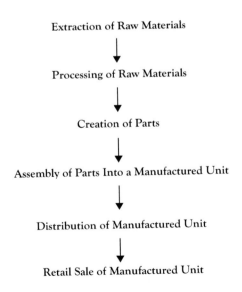

Figure 5.1. Generic value chain for a manufactured good.

Horizontal Integration

In horizontal integration, a firm either increases the volume of current production activities or expands to similar kinds of production activities. Consider a television manufacturer that operates at the assembly stage of its value chain. If that company bought out another manufacturer of television sets, this would be horizontal integration. If the company were to decide to assemble computer monitors, the product would be a form of horizontal integration due to the high similarity in the two products and type of activity within those value chains.

Cost efficiencies in the form of economies of scale from higher volumes or economies of scope from producing related products are primary driving factors in horizontal integration. When a firm expands to a new product that is similar to its current products, usually there is a transfer of knowledge and experience that allows the expanding firm to start with higher cost efficiency than a firm that is entering this market with no related experience. If an enterprise possesses core competencies in the form of production processes that it can perform as well or better than others in the market, and can identify other products that can employ those core competencies, the enterprise can enter new markets as a serious competitor.

Market power from holding a higher share of all sales in a market is the other major motivation for horizontal integration. As we will discuss in later chapters, the possible gains from increased market power are often so significant that the governments in charge of overseeing those markets may limit or forbid horizontal mergers where one company buys out or combines with a competitor.

Since most firms are buyers as well as sellers, horizontal integration can create an advantage for large firms in demanding lower prices for goods and services they purchase. For example, a national chain like Walmart may be the principal customer of one of its suppliers. If Walmart decides to use a different supplier, the former supplier may have difficulty remaining in business. Consequently, the supplier may have little choice about accepting reduced prices.

Vertical Integration

Vertical integration occurs when a firm expands into a different stage of a value chain in which it already operates. For example, suppose the television manufacturing firm had been purchasing the electronic circuit boards that it uses in its television set products but decides to either buy the supplier or start a new operation to make those parts for itself. This would be vertical integration.

Usually vertical integration will extend to a neighboring stage in the value chain. When a business expands into an earlier stage in the value chain, the business is said to be doing *upstream integration*. When the expansion is to a later stage of the value chain, the result is *downstream integration*.

A major motivation for vertical integration is the potential for improved profitability. As noted earlier, firms at some stages of the value chain may enjoy better market conditions in terms of profitability and stability. If two stages of the value chain are performed by two divisions of the same company rather than by two separate companies, there is less haggling over price and other conditions of sale. In some cases, through a process that economists call *double marginalization*,[1] it is possible that a single vertically integrated firm can realize higher profit than the total of two independent firms operating at different stages and making exchanges. An independent partner may not conduct its business the way that the firm would prefer, and possibly the only means to make sure other stages of the value chain operate as a firm would like is for the firm to actually manage the operations in those stages.

Another possible motivation for vertical integration is risk reduction. If a firm is highly dependent on the goods and services of a particular supplier or purchases by a particular buyer, the firm may find itself in jeopardy if that supplier or buyer were to suddenly decide to switch to other clients or cease operations. For example, if the supplier of electronic circuit boards were to cancel future agreements to sell parts to the television manufacturer and instead sell to a competitor that assembles television sets, the television company may not be able to respond quickly to the loss of supply and may decide it needs to either buy out the supplier or start its own electronic parts division. From the circuit board supplier's perspective, there is also risk to them if they invest in production capacity to meet the specific part designs for the television company and then the television company decides to get the circuit boards elsewhere. By having both operations within the boundaries of a single enterprise, there is little risk of unilateral action by one producer to the detriment of the other producer.

Alternatives to Vertical Integration

If the reduction of risk related to the actions of an independent supplier or buyer is a motivation for vertical integration, the firm may have alternatives to formally integrating into another stage of the value chain through use of a carefully constructed agreement with a supplier or buyer. Done correctly, these agreements can result in some of the gains a business might expect from formal integration of the other stage of value-adding activity.

If the concern is about the reliability of continued exchanges, the supplier firm can establish a long-term agreement to be the exclusive dealer to the buyer firm, or the buyer firm can contract to be the exclusive buyer from the seller firm. In the retail business, these sometimes take the form of franchise outlets, where the franchise enjoys the assurance that their product will not be sold by a competitor within a certain distance and the supplier is assured of having a retailer that features their goods exclusively.

In some cases, the concern may be about future prices. If the upstream firm is concerned that the downstream firm will charge too little and hurt their profitability, the upstream firm can insist on a resale price maintenance clause. If the downstream firm is concerned that the upstream firm will use their exchanges to build up a business and then seek additional business with other downstream clients at lower prices, the downstream firm can ask for a best price policy that guarantees them the lowest price charged to any of the upstream firm's customers.

Some upstream suppliers may produce a variety of goods and rely on downstream distributors to sell these goods to consumers. However, the downstream firm may find that selling just a portion of the upstream firm's product line is more lucrative and will not willingly distribute the upstream firm's entire line of products. If this is a concern to the upstream firm, it can insist on the composition of products a distributor will offer as a condition of being a distributor of any of its products.

One way firms protect themselves from supply shortages is by maintaining sizeable inventories of parts. However, maintaining inventory costs money. Firms that exchange goods in a value chain can reduce the need for large inventories with coordinated schedules like just-in-time systems.[2] In situations where quality of the good is of key concern, and not just the price, the downstream firm can require documentation of quality control processes in the upstream firm.

When upstream firms are concerned that they may not realize a sufficient volume of exchanges over time to justify the investment in fixed assets, the upstream firm can demand a take-or-pay contract that obligates the buyer to either fulfill its intended purchases or compensate the supplier to offset losses that will occur. This type of agreement is particularly important in the case of "specific assets" in economics, where the supplier would have no viable alternative for redeploying the fixed assets to another use.

Although some of these measures may obviate the need for a firm to expand vertically in a value chain, in some circumstances forming the necessary agreements is difficult to accomplish. This is especially the case when one party in a vertical arrangement maintains private information that can be used to its advantage to create a better deal for itself but potentially will be a bad arrangement for the party that does not have that information in advance. As a result, parties that are aware of their limited information about the other party will tend to be more conservative in their agreement terms by assuming pessimistic circumstances and will not be able to reach an agreement. This reaction is called *adverse selection* in economic literature.[3]

In some cases, one party in a vertical arrangement may have production or planning secrets that do not affect the agreement per se but risk being discovered by the other party as the result of any exchange transactions. These secrets may be the result of costly research and development but may pass to the other party at essentially no cost, and the other party may take advantage of that easily obtained information. This is a version of what economists call the free rider problem.[4] Due to the difficulty of protecting against problems of adverse selection and free riders, firms may conclude that vertical integration is the better option.

Conglomerates

As stated earlier, a conglomerate is a business enterprise that participates in multiple value chains that are different in nature. An example of a conglomerate is General Electric, which engages in the manufacture of appliances, construction of energy facilities, financing of projects, and media ventures, just to name a portion of its product portfolio.

One attraction of conglomerates is the ability to diversify so that the firm can withstand difficult times in one industry by having a presence in other kinds of markets. Beyond diversification, a conglomerate can move capital from one of its businesses to another business without the cost and difficulties of using outside capital markets. Often conglomerates will have some divisions that are cash cows in being profitable operations in mature markets, and other businesses that have great potential but require sizeable investment that can be funded by profits from the cash-cow businesses.[5]

Another argument for conglomerates is that companies with very talented management staffs may be capable of excelling in more than one type of business. For instance, the former chairman of General Electric, Jack Welch, was widely praised as providing superior senior management for the wide range of businesses in which General Electric participated.

Transaction Costs and Boundaries of the Firm

We have discussed several reasons a firm may decide to expand. At first glance, it may seem that expanding a business is often a good idea and has little downside risk if the larger enterprise is managed properly. In fact, during the last century successful businesses often engaged in horizontal and vertical integration and even became conglomerates due to such reasoning.

However, as many of these large corporations learned, it is possible to become too large, too complex, or too diversified. One consequence of a corporation growing large and complex is that it needs a management structure that is large and complex. There needs to be some specialization among managers, much as there is specialization in its labor force. Each manager only understands a small piece of the corporation's operations, so there needs to be efficient communication between managers to be able to take advantage of the opportunities of integration and conglomeration. This requires additional management to manage the managers.

Large firms usually have some form of layered or pyramid management both to allow specialization of management and to facilitate communication. Still, as the number of layers increases, the complexity of communication grows faster than the size of the management staff. Information overload results in the failure of key information to arrive to the right person at the right time. In effect, at some point the firm can experience diseconomies of scale and diseconomies of scope as the result of management complexity increasing faster than the rate of growth in the overall enterprise.

Another problem with expansion, especially in the cases of vertical integration and conglomerates, is that different kinds of businesses may do better with different styles of management. The culture of a successful manufacturer of consumer goods is not necessarily the culture of a startup software company. When many kinds of businesses are part of the same corporation, it may be difficult to synchronize different business cultures.

Economists have developed a theory called *transaction cost economics* to try to explain when a firm should expand and when it should not, or even when the firm would do better to either break apart or sell off some of its business units. A transaction cost is the cost involved in making an exchange. An exchange can be external or internal. An external exchange occurs when two separate businesses are involved, like the television manufacturer and its parts supplier in the earlier example. Prior to the actual exchange of parts for cash, there is a period in which the companies need to come to agreement on price and other terms. The external transaction costs are the costs to create and monitor this agreement.

If a firm decides to expand its boundaries to handle the exchange internally, there are new internal transaction costs. These would be the costs to plan and coordinate these internal exchanges. If exchanges of this nature have not been done before, these internal transaction costs can be significant.

Nobel Prize laureate Ronald Coase introduced the concept of transaction costs and also proposed a principle for determining when to expand known as the Coase hypothesis.[6] Essentially, the principle states that firms should continue to expand as long as internal transaction costs are less than external transaction costs for the same kind of exchange.

Cost Centers Versus Profit Centers

One internal transaction cost in multiple-division companies is how to coordinate the divisions that make internal exchanges so they will achieve what is best for the overall corporation. This challenge is not merely a matter of communication but of providing proper motivation for the individual units.

Large vertically integrated companies often have at least one upstream division that creates a product and a downstream division that distributes it or sells it to consumers. One design for such companies is to have a central upper management that decides what activities and activity levels should be provided by each division. These instructions are given to the division managers. With the output goals of each division established, each division will best contribute to the overall profitability of the corporation by trying to meet its output goals at minimum cost. As such, divisions operating under this philosophy are called cost centers.

Although the cost center design may sound workable in principle, there is some risk in the division having an overall objective of minimizing cost and divisional management evaluated in terms of that objective. The response to this objective is that the firm may cut corners on quality as much as possible and avoid considering innovations that would incur higher initial costs but ultimately result in a better product for the long run. Unless the top-level management is aware of these issues and sets quality requirements properly, opportunities may be missed.

Another problem with cost centers, particularly in the nonprofit and public sectors, is that the compensation and prestige afforded to division managers may be related to the size of division operations. Consequently, the incentive for managers is to try to justify larger cost budgets rather than limit costs.

An alternative to the cost center approach is to treat a division as if it were like a business that had its own revenues and costs. The goal of each division is to create the most value in terms of the difference between its revenues and costs. This is known as a profit center. Division managers of profit centers not only have incentives to avoid waste and improve efficiencies like cost centers but also have an incentive to improve the product in ways that create better value.

Transfer Pricing

The profit center model treats a corporate division as if it were an autonomous business within a business. However, often the reason for having multiple divisions in an enterprise is because there is vertical integration, meaning that some divisions are providing goods and services to other divisions in the enterprise. If the two divisions in an exchange are to be treated as if they were separate businesses, what price should be charged by the supplying division? Even if there is no actual cash being tendered by the acquiring division, some measurement of value for the exchange is needed to serve as the revenue for the selling division and the cost for the acquiring division. The established value assigned to the exchanged item is called a *transfer price*.

One possibility for establishing a transfer price is for the two divisions to negotiate a price as they would if they were indeed independent businesses. Unfortunately, this approach sacrifices one of the benefits of vertical integration—namely, the avoidance of the transaction costs that are incurred on external changes—without avoiding all the internal transaction costs.

Another approach to the problem of pricing interdivision exchanges is to base prices on principles rather than negotiation. Academic research has concluded a number of principles for different kinds of situations. In this section, we will limit our consideration to two of these situations.

Suppose two divisions in an enterprise, Division A and Division B, exchange a good that is only produced by Division A. More specifically, there is no other division either inside or outside the enterprise that currently produces the good. Division B is the only user of this good, either inside or outside of the enterprise. Under these conditions, theoretically the best transfer price is the marginal cost of the good incurred by Division A.

No formal proof of this principle will be offered here, but a brief defense of this principle would be as follows: Suppose the price charged was less than the marginal cost. If Division A decides on the production volume that would maximize its internal divisional profit, then by reducing its volume somewhat, Division A would avoid more cost than it loses in forgone transfer revenue. So Division A would elect to provide fewer units than Division B would want.

On the other hand, suppose the transfer price was set at a level higher than the marginal cost. Since the transfer cost becomes a component of cost to receiving Division B, in determining its optimal volume of production, Division B will see a higher marginal cost than is actually the case (or would be the case if Divisions A and B functioned as a single unit). As a result, Division B may decide on a production level that is not optimal for the overall enterprise. By setting the transfer price equal to Division A's marginal cost, the decision by Division B should be the same as it would be if the two divisions operated as one.

Although the principle is reasonably clear and defensible in theory, the participating divisions in an actual setting may raise objections. If the average cost of the item to Division A is less than the marginal cost, Division B may complain that they should not need to pay a transfer price above the average cost because that is what the actual cost per item is to Division A and the enterprise overall. If the average cost per item exceeds the marginal cost, Division A may complain that setting the transfer price to the marginal cost requires their division to operate at a loss for this item and they should be credited with at least the average cost. Nonetheless, the best decisions by Divisions A and B for the overall profit of the enterprise will occur when the transfer price is based on the marginal cost to Division A in this situation.

As a second case situation, suppose the good transferred from Division A to Division B is a good that is both produced and consumed outside the enterprise and there is a highly competitive market for both buyers and sellers. In this instance the best internal transfer price between Division A and Division B would be the external market price.

A supporting argument for this principle is this: If the transfer price were higher than the outside market price, Division B could reduce its costs by purchasing the good in the outside market rather than obtaining it from Division A. If the outside market price were higher than the set transfer price, Division A would make higher divisional profit by selling the good on the outside market than by transferring it to Division B.

Employee Motivation

Earlier we considered how to motivate divisions within a large organization with appropriate transfer pricing. How about motivation within the divisions? As noted in the introduction to this chapter, in recent decades economists have addressed this matter from a new perspective.

The traditional approach to motivation inside a division or modest-sized business was typically regarded as matters of organizational design and organizational behavior. Once the employee agreed to employment in return for salary or wages and benefits, his services were subject to direction by management within the scope of human resource policies in terms of hours worked and work conditions. Ensuring good performance by employees was basically a matter of appropriate supervision, encouragement, and feedback. In cases where employees were not performing adequately, they would be notified of the problem, possibly disciplined, or even dismissed and replaced. From this perspective, managing employees is much like managing military troops, differing largely in terms of the degree of control on the individual's free time and movements.

The new perspective on employee motivation is to consider the employee more like an individual contractor rather than an enlisted soldier. Just as microeconomics viewed each consumer as an entity trying to maximize the utility for his household, an individual employee is a decision-making unit who agrees to an employment relationship if he believes this is the best utilization of his productive abilities. The challenge for business management is to structure compensation, incentives, and personnel policies that induce employees to contribute near their productive capacities but not overreward employees beyond what makes economic sense for the business.

One contribution from this economic perspective is the notion of an *efficiency wage*.[7] The classical approach to setting wages is that the wage paid to an employee should be no more than the marginal revenue product corresponding to her effort. However, if an employee is paid barely what her efforts are worth to the firm at the margin and if there is a competitive market for the employee's services in other firms, the employee may not be motivated to work at maximum capacity or avoid engaging in behaviors that are detrimental to the firm because she can earn as much elsewhere if she is dismissed. An efficiency wage is a wage that is set somewhat above the marginal revenue product of the employee to give the employee an incentive to be productive and retain this job because the employee would sacrifice the difference between the efficiency wage and marginal revenue product if she sought employment elsewhere. This incentive is worthwhile to the firm because it avoids the transaction costs of finding and hiring a new employee.

Another contribution of this economic viewpoint of employee motivation is an examination of employee contracts to deal with what is called the *principal-agent problem*. In this context, the hiring business is a principal that hires an employee (agent) to act on its behalf. The problem occurs when the agent is motivated to take actions that are not necessarily what the employer would want, but the employer is not able to monitor all the activities of the employee and has insufficient information.

In the employment relationship the employer evaluates the employee on the basis of her contribution to profit or other objective of the firm. However, the employee evaluates her activities based on the amount of effort involved. To the degree that employees see their compensation and incentives connected to the intensity of effort, the more likely the employee will invest additional effort because there is reduced risk that her efforts will go unrewarded.

For example, if employee incentives are based on the overall performance of a team of employees without any discrimination between individual employees, there is an incentive for employees to shirk in performance of their jobs because they still benefit if others do the work and they do not risk putting in an extra effort to see the reward diminished by sharing the incentives with others who did not put in the same effort. The *informativeness principle* suggests that measures of performance that reflect individual employee effort be included in employee contracts.[8]

A third interesting contribution of this perspective on employee motivation is the concept of *signaling*.[9] When employers hire, they face a pool of possible employees. Some employees will perform well, whereas others will not due to either lack of skills or lack of character. In the interview process, the employer will try to assess which applicants will be good employees, but these evaluation processes are imperfect. The real intentions of the applicant if and when he becomes an employee are largely private information until the person is actually hired and on the job for a while. As a result, employers face an *adverse selection* problem similar to what was discussed earlier in the context of vertical integration and will often protect against the risk by lowering the compensation offered, even though they would be willing to pay a motivated, qualified employee more.

One response to the adverse selection problem by the employee is to take actions on his own that will help distinguish him from others in the applicant pool, which are observable and serve as a signal to the employer. Seeking a college degree has been cited as a kind of signal. Even though much of what the employee learned as part of obtaining the college degree may be of little use in the prospective employment relationship, the fact that the applicant was willing to endure the cost and effort for a college degree, particularly a degree supported with good grades, is evidence that the applicant is more likely to be a dedicated and competent employee.

Applicants for employment or hire often have several employment relationships over time. By attaching importance to reputation, employers can both motivate employees to be more diligent in their current positions and establish a mechanism to help distinguish high-quality workers from low-quality workers in future hiring.

Manager Motivation and Executive Pay

In businesses where the manager is not the owner, there is another manifestation of the principal-agent problem. For example, in a typical corporation, the owners are stockholders, many of whom are not involved in the actual production activities. The board of directors hires executive management to act as the agents of the shareholders, who are the principals in this context. The intent of the arrangement is that the executives will manage the corporation in the best long-term interests of the shareholders. However, the executives, though they may own some of the corporation's shares, are largely rewarded via salaries, bonuses, and other perquisites. Structuring executive contracts that both motivate the executive and represent the owners' interests is a challenge.

The executives in corporations are often paid highly, certainly well above the opportunity cost of their labor in a nonexecutive setting. There are multiple theories for these high executive salaries. One argument is based on economic rent, namely, that talented executives are like star athletes and art performers, being in relatively short supply, so corporations must pay well above their opportunity cost to have their services.

Another argument for high executive pay is that they need to be not only compensated for their effort but rewarded for the value they create on behalf of the owners. So part of the higher salary is a share of the profits resulting from their execution of management duties.

A third argument for high executive salaries is that firms must often take significant risks to succeed in competitive markets and uncertain conditions. If the firm fails or falls short when its performance is assessed after the fact, the executive may lose his job. In response to this, the executive may avoid bold moves that have a significant risk of failure. In paying an executive highly, the executive is compensated for the additional personal risk he assumes by being willing to take reasonable chances that the corporation must tolerate.

Another interesting argument for high executive pay is called *tournament theory*.[10] This applies to large enterprises with a sizeable team of executives, with a highly paid chief executive officer (CEO), along with several other vice presidents who are in line for consideration to become a future CEO. By paying the CEO generously and well beyond what is economically justifiable on the basis of the CEO's contributions *per se*, there is a strong incentive for the other executives to put in extra effort so they will become that chief executive, with all the high pay and perquisites, in the future. From the perspective of the shareholders, the gain from those collective extra efforts is worth the high salary to the last winner of the CEO "tournament."

CHAPTER 6

Market Equilibrium and the Perfect Competition Model

The remaining chapters of this text are devoted to the operations of markets. In economics, a *market* refers to the collective activity of buyers and sellers for a particular product or service.

In this chapter we will focus on what might be considered the gold standard of a market: the perfect competition model. The operations of actual markets deviate from the perfect competition model, sometimes substantially. Still, this model serves as both a good initial framework for describing how a market functions and a reference base for evaluating any market.

Assumptions of the Perfect Competition Model

The perfect competition model is built on five assumptions:

1. The market consists of many buyers. Any single buyer represents a very small fraction of all the purchases in a market. Due to its insignificant impact on the market, the buyer acts as a *price taker*, meaning the buyer presumes her purchase decision has no impact on the price charged for the good. The buyer takes the price as given and decides the amount to purchase that best serves the utility of her household.

2. The market consists of many sellers. Any single seller represents a very small fraction of all the purchases in a market. Due to its insignificant impact on the market, the seller acts as a *price taker*, meaning the seller presumes its production decisions have no impact on the price charged for the good by other sellers. The seller takes the price as given and decides the amount to produce that will generate the greatest profit.

3. Firms that sell in the market are free to either enter or exit the market. Firms that are not currently sellers in the market may enter as sellers if they find the market attractive. Firms currently selling in the market may discontinue participation as sellers if they find the market unattractive. Existing firms may also continue to participate at different production levels as conditions change.

4. The good sold by all sellers in the market is assumed to be *homogeneous*. This means every seller sells the same good, or stated another way, the buyer does not care which seller he uses if all sellers charge the same price.

5. Buyers and sellers in the market are assumed to have *perfect information*. Producers understand the production capabilities known to other producers in the market and have immediate access to any resources used by other sellers in producing a good. Both buyers and sellers know all the prices being charged by other sellers.

Operation of a Perfectly Competitive Market in the Short Run

The consequence of the preceding assumptions is that all exchanges in a perfectly competitive market will quickly converge to a single price. Since the good is viewed as being of identical quality and utility, regardless of the seller, and the buyers have perfect information about seller prices, if one seller is charging less than another seller, no buyer will purchase from the higher priced seller. As a result, all sellers that elect to remain in the market will quickly settle at charging the same price.

In chapters 2 and 3, we examined the demand curves seen by a firm. In the case of the perfect competition model, since sellers are price takers and their presence in the market is of small consequence, the demand curve they see is a flat curve, such that they can produce and sell any quantity between zero and their production limit for the next period, but the price will remain constant (see Figure 6.1).

It must be noted that although each firm in the market perceives a flat demand curve, the demand curve representing the behavior of all buyers in the market need not be a flat line. Since some buyers will value the item more than others and even individual buyers will have decreasing utility for

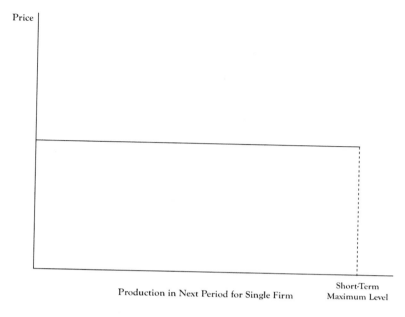

Figure 6.1. Flat demand curve as seen by an individual seller in a perfectly competitive market. Any amount the firm offers for sale during a production period (up to its maximum possible production level) will sell at the market price.

additional units of the item, the total market demand curve will generally take the shape of a downward sloping curve, such as Figure 6.2.

The downward sloping nature of the market demand curve in Figure 6.2 may seem to contradict the flat demand curve for a single firm depicted in Figure 6.1. This difference can be explained by the fact that any single seller is viewed as being a very small component of the market. Whether a single firm operated at its maximum possible level or dropped out entirely, the impact on the overall market price or total market quantity would be negligible.

Although all firms will be forced to charge the same price under perfect competition and firms have perfect information about the production technologies of other firms, firms may not be identical in the short run. Some may have lower costs or higher capacities. Consequently, not all firms will earn the same amount of profit.

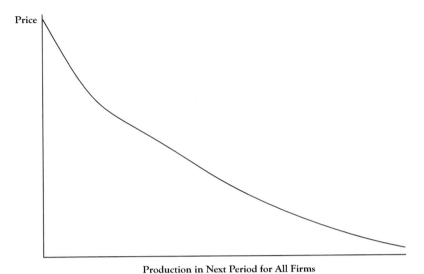

Production in Next Period for All Firms

Figure 6.2. Demand curve as seen for all sellers in a market.
Although one seller sees a fixed price for its supply, if all sellers were
to increase production, the maximum price that customers would pay
to buy all the units offered would drop.

As described in the description of the shutdown rule in chapter 2, some firms only operate at an economic profit because they have considerable sunk costs that are not considered in determining whether it is profitable to operate in the short run. Thus not only are there differences in profits among firms in the short run, but even if the market price were to remain the same, not all the firms would be able to justify remaining in the market when their fixed costs need to be replenished, unless they were able to adapt their production to match the more successful operators.

Perfect Competition in the Long Run

As described in chapter 4, a long-run time frame for a producer is enough time for the producer to implement any changes to its processes. In the short run, there may be differences in size and production processes of the firms selling in the market. Some sellers may be able to make a healthy economic profit, whereas others may only barely make enough to justify continued operation and, as noted earlier, may not have sustainable operations although they may continue to operate for a while since a substantial portion of their short-run costs are sunk costs.

Due to the assumption of perfect information, all sellers know the production techniques of their competitors. As a result, any firm that intends to remain in the market will revise its operations to mimic the operations of the most successful firms in the market. In theory, in the long run all firms would either have the most cost-efficient operations or abandon the market.

However, when all firms use the same processes, the possibility for firms to continue to earn positive economic profits will disappear. Suppose all firms are earning a positive profit at the going market price. One firm will see the opportunity to drop its price a small amount, still be able to earn an economic profit, and with the freedom to redefine itself in the long run, no longer be constrained by short-run production limits. Of course, when one firm succeeds in gaining greater profit by cutting its prices, the other firms will have no choice but to follow or exit the market, since buyers in perfect competition will only be willing to purchase the good from the seller who has the lowest price. Since the price has been lowered, all firms will have a lower economic profit than they had collectively before they lowered the price.

Some firms may realize they can even drive the price lower, again take sales from their competitors, and increase economic profit. Once again, all firms will be required to follow their lead or drop out of the market because firms that do not drop the price again will lose all their customers. And once again, as all firms match the lowered price, the economic profits are diminished.

In theory, due to competition, homogeneous goods, and perfect information, firms will continue to match and undercut other firms on the price, until the price drops to the point where all remaining firms make an economic profit of zero. As we explained earlier, an economic profit of zero is sufficient to sustain operations, but the firm will no longer be earning an accounting profit beyond the opportunity costs of the resources employed in their ventures.

Another necessary development in the long run under perfect competition is that all firms will need to be large enough to reach minimum efficient scale. Recall from chapter 4 that minimum efficient scale is the minimum production rate necessary to get the average cost per item as low as possible. Firms operating at minimum efficient scale could charge a price equal to that minimum average cost and still be viable. Smaller firms with higher average costs will not be able to compete because they will have losses if they charge those prices yet will lose customers to the large firms with lower prices if they do not match their prices. So, in the long run, firms that have operations smaller than minimum efficient scale will need to either grow to at least minimum efficient scale or leave the market.

Firm Supply Curves and Market Supply Curves

The demand curve describes how either one consumer or a group of consumers would change the amount they would purchase if the price were to change. Producers may also adjust the amounts they sell if the market price changes.

Recall from chapter 2 the principle that a firm should operate in the short run if they can achieve an economic profit; otherwise the firm should shut down in the short run. If the firm decides it is profitable to operate, another principle from chapter 2 stated that the firm should increase production up to the level where marginal cost equals marginal revenue.

In the case of a flat demand curve, the marginal revenue to a firm is equal to the market price. Based on this principle, we can prescribe the best operating level for the firm in response to the market price as follows:

- If the price is too low to earn an economic profit at any possible operating level, shut down.
- If the price is higher than the marginal cost when production is at the maximum possible level in the short run, the firm should operate at that maximum level.
- Otherwise, the firm should operate at the level where price is equal to marginal cost.

Figure 6.3 shows a generic situation with average (economic) cost and marginal cost curves. Based on the preceding rule, a relationship between the market price and the optimal quantity supplied is the segment of the marginal cost curve that is above the shutdown price level and where the

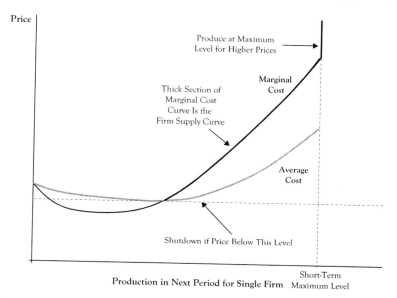

Figure 6.3. Relationship of average cost curve, marginal cost curve, and firm supply curve for a single seller in a perfectly competitive market.

marginal cost curve is increasing, up to the point of maximum production. For prices higher than the marginal cost at maximum production, the firm would operate at maximum production.

This curve segment provides an analogue to the demand curve to describe the best response of sellers to market prices and is called the *firm supply curve.* As is done with demand curves, the convention in economics is to place the quantity on the horizontal axis and price on the vertical axis. Note that although demand curves are typically downward sloping to reflect that consumers' utility for a good diminishes with increased consumption, firm supply curves are generally upward sloping. The upward sloping character reflects that firms will be willing to increase production in response to a higher market price because the higher price may make additional production profitable. Due to differences in capacities and production technologies, seller firms may have different firm supply curves.

If we were to examine all firm supply curves to determine the total quantity that sellers would provide at any given price and determined the relationship between the total quantity provided and the market price, the result would be the *market supply curve*. As with firm supply curves, market supply curves are generally upward sloping and reflect both the willingness of firms to push production higher in relation to improved profitability and the willingness of some firms to come out of a short-run shutdown when the price improves sufficiently.

Market Equilibrium

The market demand curve indicates the maximum price that buyers will pay to purchase a given quantity of the market product. The market supply curve indicates the minimum price that suppliers would accept to be willing to provide a given supply of the market product. In order to have buyers and sellers agree on the quantity that would be provided and purchased, the price needs to be a right level.

The *market equilibrium* is the quantity and associated price at which there is concurrence between sellers and buyers. If the market demand curve and market supply curve are displayed on the same graph, the market equilibrium occurs at the point where the two curves intersect (see Figure 6.4).

Recall that the perfect competition model assumes all buyers and sellers in the market are price takers. This raises an interesting question: If all the actors in the market take the price as given condition, how does the market get to an equilibrium price?

One answer to this question was provided by the person who is often described as the first economist, Adam Smith. Adam Smith lived in the late 18th century, many years before a formal field of economics was recognized. In his own time, Smith was probably regarded as a philosopher. He wrote a treatise called *The Wealth of Nations*,[1] in which he attempted to explain the prosperity that erupted in Europe as the result of expanded commercial trade and the industrial revolution.

Smith ascribed the mechanism that moves a market to equilibrium as a force he called the *invisible hand*. In effect, if the price is not at the equilibrium level, sellers will detect an imbalance between supply and demand and some will be motivated to test other prices. If existing market price is below the equilibrium price, the provided supply will be insufficient to meet the demand. Sensing this, some suppliers will try a slightly higher

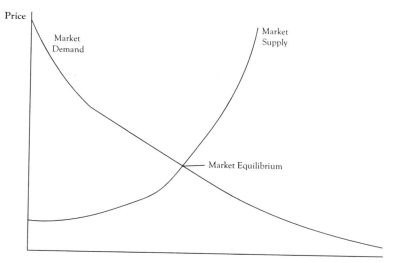

Figure 6.4. Market equilibrium as the coordinates for quantity and price where the market demand curve crosses the market supply curve.

price and learn that, despite perfect information among buyers, some buyers will be willing to pay the higher price if an additional amount would be supplied. Other sellers will see that the higher price has enough demand and raise their prices as well. The new price may still be below equilibrium, so a few sellers will test a higher price again, and the process will repeat until there is no longer a perception of excess demand beyond the amount buyers want at the current price.

If the market price is higher than the equilibrium price, sellers will initially respond with increased rates of production but will realize that buyers are not willing to purchase all the goods available. Some sellers will consider lowering the price slightly to make a sale of goods that would otherwise go unsold. Seeing this is successful in encouraging more demand, and due to buyers being able to shift their consumption to the lower priced sellers, all sellers will be forced to accept the lower price. As a result, some sellers will produce less based on the change in their firm supply curve and other sellers may shut down entirely, so the total market supply will contract. This process may be repeated until the price lowers to the level where the quantity supplied is in equilibrium with the quantity demanded.

In actual markets, equilibrium is probably more a target toward which prices and market quantity move rather than a state that is achieved. Further, the equilibrium itself is subject to change due to events that change the demand behavior of buyers and production economics of suppliers. Changes in climate, unexpected outages, and accidental events are examples of factors that can alter the market equilibrium. As a result, the market price and quantity is often in a constant state of flux, due to both usually being out of equilibrium and trying to reach an equilibrium that is itself a moving target.

Shifts in Supply and Demand Curves

In addition to the factors that cause fluctuations in the market equilibrium, some developments may lead to sustained changes in the market equilibrium. For example, if a new product becomes available that is a viable substitute for an existing product, there is likely to be either a persistent drop in the quantity consumed of the existing good or a reduction in the market price for the existing good.

The impact of these persistent changes can be viewed in the context of changes in the behavior of buyers or the operations of sellers that cause a shift in the demand curve or the supply curve, respectively. In the case of the new availability of a close substitute for an existing product, we would expect the demand curve to shift to the left, indicating that at any market price for the existing good, demand will be less than it was prior to introduction of the substitute. As another example, consider the supply curve for gasoline after an increase in the price of crude oil. Since the cost of producing a gallon of gasoline will increase, the marginal cost of gasoline will increase at any level of production and the result will be an upward shift in the supply curve.

It is often of interest to determine the impact of a changing factor on the market equilibrium. Will the equilibrium quantity increase or decrease? Will the equilibrium price increase or decrease? Will the shift in the equilibrium point be more of a change in price or a change in quantity? The examination of the impact of a change on the equilibrium point is known in economics as *comparative statics*.

In the case of a shifting demand curve, since the supply curve is generally upward sloping, a shift of the demand curve either upward or to
the right will result in both a higher equilibrium price and equilibrium
quantity. Likewise, a shift in the demand curve either downward or to
the left will usually result in a lower equilibrium price and a lower equilibrium quantity. So in response to the introduction of a new substitute
good where we would expect a leftward shift in the demand curve, both
the equilibrium price and quantity for the existing good can be expected
to decrease (see Figure 6.5).

Whether a shift in the demand curve results in a greater relative
change in the equilibrium price or the equilibrium quantity depends on
the shape of the supply curve. If the supply curve is fairly flat, or elastic, the change will be primarily in the equilibrium quantity (see Figure
6.6a). An elastic supply curve means that a small change in price typically
results in a greater response in the provided quantity. If the supply curve
is fairly vertical, or inelastic, the change in equilibrium will be mostly
seen as a price change (see Figure 6.6b).

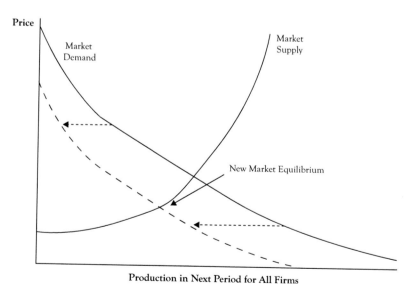

Production in Next Period for All Firms

*Figure 6.5. Shift of market demand to the left in response to a new
substitute and change in the market equilibrium.*

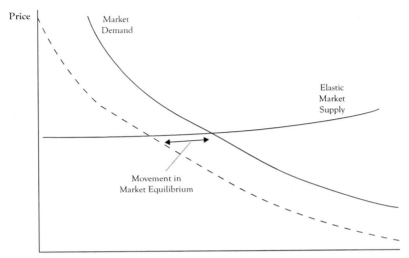

Figure 6.6a. Impact of elasticity of the supply curve on the impact of a shift in the demand curve. The shift is generally in terms of the quantity when the supply curve is elastic.

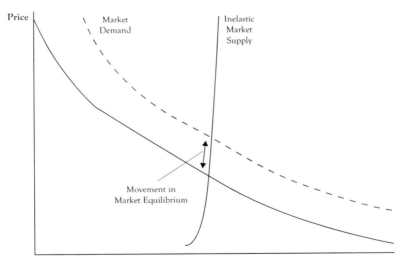

Figure 6.6b. Impact of elasticity of the supply curve on the impact of a shift in the demand curve. The shift is generally in terms of the price when the supply curve is inelastic.

A shift in the supply curve has a different effect on the equilibrium. Because the demand curve is generally downward sloping, a shift in the supply curve either upward or to the left will result in a higher equilibrium price and a lower equilibrium quantity. However, a shift in the supply either downward or to the right will result in a lower equilibrium price and a higher equilibrium quantity. So for the example of the gasoline market where the supply curve shifts upward, we can expect prices to rise and the quantity sold to decrease (see Figure 6.7).

The shape of the demand curve dictates whether a shift in the supply curve will result in more change in the equilibrium price or the equilibrium quantity. With a demand curve that is flat, or elastic, a shift in supply curve will change the equilibrium quantity more than the price (see Figure 6.8a). With a demand curve that is vertical, or inelastic, a shift in the supply curve will change the equilibrium price more than the equilibrium quantity (see Figure 6.8b).

The characterization of a demand curve as being elastic or inelastic corresponds to the measure of price elasticity that was discussed in chapter 3. Recall from the discussion of short-run versus long-run demand that in the short run, customers are limited in their options by their

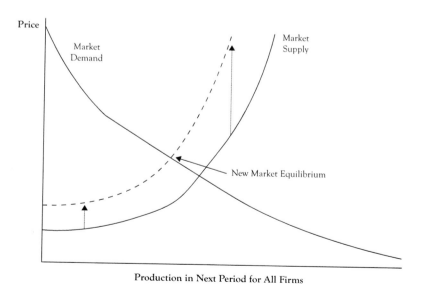

Production in Next Period for All Firms

Figure 6.7. Shift of market supply upward in response to an increase in the price of crude oil and change in the market equilibrium.

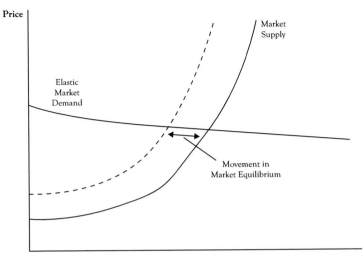

Figure 6.8a. Impact of elasticity of the demand curve on the impact of a shift in the supply curve. The shift is generally in terms of the quantity when the demand curve is elastic.

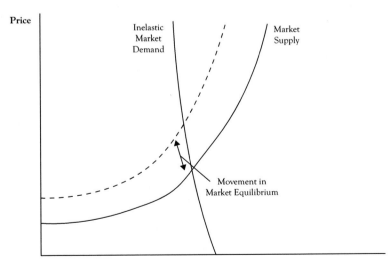

Figure 6.8b. Impact of elasticity of the demand curve on the impact of a shift in the supply curve. The shift is generally in terms of the price when the demand curve is inelastic.

consumption patterns and technologies. This is particularly true in the case of gasoline consumption. Consequently, short-run demand curves for gasoline tend to be very inelastic. As a result, if changing crude oil prices results in an upward shift in the supply curve for gasoline, we should expect the result to be a substantial increase in the price of gasoline and only a fairly modest decrease in the amount of gasoline consumed.

Why Perfect Competition Is Desirable

In a simple market under perfect competition, equilibrium occurs at a quantity and price where the marginal cost of attracting one more unit from one supplier is equal to the highest price that will attract the purchase of one more unit from a buyer. At the price charged at equilibrium, some buyers are getting a bargain of sorts because they would have been willing to purchase at least some units even if the price had been somewhat higher. The fact that market demand curves are downward sloping rather than perfectly flat reflects willingness of customers to make purchases at higher prices.

At least in theory, we could imagine taking all the units that would be purchased at the equilibrium price and using the location of each unit purchase on the demand curve to determine the maximum amount that the buyer would have been willing to pay to purchase that unit. The difference between what the customer would have paid to buy a unit and the lower equilibrium price he actually paid constitutes a kind of surplus that goes to the buyer. If we determined this surplus for each item purchased and accumulated the surplus, we would have a quantity called *consumer surplus*. Using a graph of a demand curve, we can view consumer surplus as the area under the demand curve down to the horizontal line corresponding to the price being charged, as shown in Figure 6.9.

On the supplier side, there is also a potential for a kind of surplus. Since market supply curves are usually upward sloping, there are some sellers who would have been willing to sell the product even if the price had been lower because the marginal cost of the item was below the market price, and in perfect competition, a producer will always sell another item if the price is at least as high as the marginal cost. If, as before, we assessed each item sold in terms of its marginal cost, calculated the difference between the price and the marginal cost, and then accumulated those differences, the sum would be a quantity called the *producer surplus*.

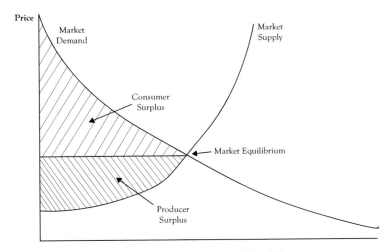

Production in Next Period for All Firms

Figure 6.9. Graph of market demand and market supply curves showing the consumer surplus and producer surplus when the market is in perfect competition equilibrium.

The producer surplus reflects the combined economic profit of all sellers in the short run. For a graph of the supply curve, the producer surplus corresponds to the area above the supply curve up to the horizontal line at the market price, again as shown in Figure 6.9.

Consumer surplus will increase as the price gets lower (assuming sellers are willing to supply at the level on the demand curve) and producer surplus will increase as the prices gets higher (assuming buyers are willing to purchase the added amount as you move up the supply curve). If we asked the question, at what price would the sum of consumer surplus plus producer surplus would be greatest, the answer is at the equilibrium price, where the demand curve and supply curve cross.

To support this claim, suppose sellers decided to increase the price above the equilibrium price. Since consumers would purchase fewer items, the quantity they could sell is dictated by the demand curve. The new producer surplus, as seen in Figure 6.10, might be higher than the producer surplus at the equilibrium price, but the consumer surplus would be decidedly lower. So any increase in producer surplus comes from what had been consumer surplus. However, there is a triangular area in Figure 6.10, between the supply and demand curve and to the right of the new quantity level, which represents former surplus that no longer goes to either consumers or producers. Economists call this lost surplus a *deadweight loss.*

If the price were lower than the equilibrium price, we encounter a situation where producer surplus decreases and at best only some of that decrease transfers to consumers. The rest of the lost producer surplus is again a deadweight loss, as seen in Figure 6.11.

The important point is that changing the price is worse than just a shift of surplus from consumers to producers, or vice versa. If the entire sum of consumer surplus and producer surplus could grow at a different price, it could be argued that the government could use a tax to take some of the excess received by one group and redistribute it to the other party so everyone was as well off or better off. Unfortunately, due to the deadweight loss, the gain to one of two parties will not offset the loss to the other party. So the equilibrium point is not only a price and quantity where we have agreement between the demand curve and supply curve, but also the point at which the greatest collective surplus is realized.

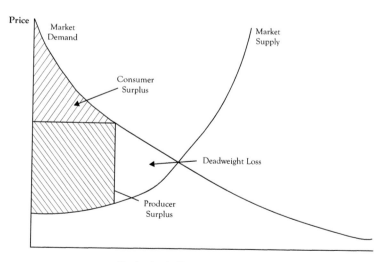

Figure 6.10. Change in consumer surplus and producer surplus when sellers increase price above the equilibrium price. Note the creation of a deadweight loss that was formerly part of either consumer surplus or producer surplus when the market operated at the perfect competition equilibrium.

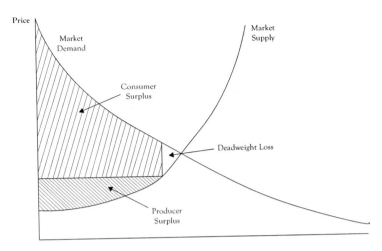

Figure 6.11. Change in consumer surplus and producer surplus when buyers force the price below the equilibrium price. Note the creation of a deadweight loss that was formerly part of either consumer surplus or producer surplus when the market operated at the perfect competition equilibrium.

Monopolistic Competition

Next we will consider some slight variations on the perfect competition model. The first is the oddly named *monopolistic competition* model,[2] which uses the same assumptions as the perfect competition model with one difference: The good sold may be heterogeneous. This means that while all sellers in the market sell a similar good that serves the same basic need of the consumer, some sellers can make slight variations in their version of the good sold in the market.

As an example, consider midsized passenger automobiles. Some firms may sell cars that are a different color or different shape, have different configurations of onboard electronics like GPS systems, and so on. Some firms may make the cars more reliable or built to last longer.

Variation in the product by sellers will only make sense if consumers are responsive to these differences and are willing to pay a slightly higher price for the variation they prefer. The reason that slightly higher prices will be necessary is that in order to support variation in product supplied, sellers may no longer be able to operate at the same minimum efficient scale that was possible when there was one version of the good that every seller produced in a manner that was indistinguishable from the good of other sellers.

The fact that firms may be able to charge a higher price may suggest that firms can now have sustained positive economic profits, particularly if they have a variation of the product that is preferred by a sizeable group of buyers. Unfortunately, even under monopolistic competition, firms can expect to do no better than a zero economic profit in the long run. The rationale for this is as follows: Suppose a firm has discovered a niche variation that is able to sustain a premium price and earn a positive economic profit. Another firm selling in the market or a new entrant in the market will be attracted to mimic the successful firm. Due to free entry and perfect information, the successful firm will not be able to stop the copycats. Once the copycats are selling a copy of this product variation, a process of price undercutting will commence as was described for perfect information, and prices will continue to drop until the price equals average cost and firms are earning only a zero economic profit.

Contestable Market Model

The *contestable market model*[3] alters a different assumption of the perfect competition model: the existence of many sellers, each of which is a barely discernable portion of all sales in the market. When we consider most of the markets that exist in the real world, it is rare that this condition of the perfect competition model applies. Rather, most markets have sellers that represent a substantial presence and would noticeably change the market if any one of them would suddenly suspend production and sales. Also, in many industries, the minimum efficient scale is so large that any firm that manages to increase to that size will be necessarily contributing a substantial fraction of all market sales.

In the contestable market model, there can be a modest number of sellers, each of which represents a sizeable portion of overall market sales. However, the assumptions of free entry and exit and perfect information need to be retained and play a key role in the theory underlying this model. If buyers in the market know which seller has the lowest price and will promptly transfer their business to the lowest price seller, once again any firm trying to sell at a higher price will lose all its customers or will need to match the lowest price.

Of course, it may be argued that the selling firms, by virtue of their size and being of limited number, could all agree to keep prices above their average cost so they can sustain positive economic profits. However, here is where the assumption of free entry spoils the party. A new entrant could see the positive economic profits of the existing sellers, enter the market at a slightly lower price, and still earn an economic profit. Once it is clear that firms are unable to sustain a pact to maintain above cost prices, price competition will drive the price to where firms will get zero economic profits.

In the late 1970s, the U.S. government changed its policy on the passenger airline market from a tightly regulated market with few approved air carriers to a deregulated market open to new entrants. The belief that airlines could behave as a contestable market model was the basis for this change. Previously, the philosophy was that airline operations required too much capital to sustain more than a small number of companies, so it was better to limit the number of commercial passenger airlines and regulate them. The change in the 1970s was that consumers would benefit by allowing free entry and exit in the passenger air travel market. Initially, the change resulted in several new airlines and increases in the ranges of operations for existing airlines, as well as more flight options and lower airfares for consumers. After a time, however, some of the larger airlines were able to thwart free entry by dominating airport gates and controlling proprietary reservation systems, causing a departure from the contestable market model.[4]

Firm Strategies in Highly Competitive Markets

Markets that closely resemble the perfect competition model or its variants might be ideal from the standpoint of market customers and as a means of increasing social surplus. From the perspective of individual selling firms, highly competitive markets require that sellers carefully attend to cost and market conditions, while promising only modest returns on assets and invested capital for those firms that manage to survive. Despite the limited opportunity for profit in these markets over the long run, good and well-executed strategies can help firms in these markets be among the survivors and perhaps extend the period in which they can do better than sell products at average cost.

Michael Porter of Harvard University prepared a guidebook for firms to prevail in these competitive markets in his text *Competitive Strategy*.[5] Basically, he advises that firms adopt an aggressive program to either keep their costs below the costs of other sellers (called a cost leadership strategy) or keep their products distinguishable from the competition (called a product differentiation strategy). The logic of either of these strategies can be viewed as trying to delay the development of the assumed conditions of perfect competition, so as to delay its long-run conclusions of zero economic profit.

The perfect competition model allows that some firms will do better than others in the short run by being able to produce a good or service at lower cost, due to having better cost management, production technologies, or economies of scale or scope. However, the model assumption of perfect information means that any firms with cost advantages will soon be discovered and mimicked. The cost leadership strategy prescribes that firms need to continually look for ways to continue to drive costs down, so that by the time the competition copies their technology and practices, they have already progressed to an even lower average cost. To succeed, these programs need to be ongoing, not just done once.

The monopolistic competition model allows for some differentiation in a product and the opportunity to charge a higher price because buyers are willing to pay a premium for this. However, any short-run opportunity for increased economic profit from selling a unique version of the product will dissipate as the competition takes notice and copies the successful variant. Porter's product differentiation strategy is basically a steady pursuit of new product variants that will be prized by the consumer, with the intent of extending the opportunity for above-normal profits. However, as with the cost leadership strategy, to be successful, a firm must commit itself to continued product differentiation with up-front investment in development and market research.

Porter suggests that each of his two strategies may be geared toward participation in a broader market or limited to a particular segment of the market, which he calls a focus strategy. A focus strategy endeavors to take advantage of market segmentation. As we discussed in chapter 3, the population of buyers is not usually homogeneous; some are willing to pay a higher price (less price elastic) and some are willing to purchase in greater volume. By focusing on a particular segment, a firm may be able to maintain an advantage over other sellers and again forestall the onset of the long-run limitations on seller profits. The goal of the focus strategy is to be able to serve this segment either at lower cost or with product variations that are valued by the customer segment. Of course, by focusing on just one or a subset of buyer segments, a firm loses the opportunity for profits in other segments, so depending on the product, the circumstances of the market, and the assets of the firm, a broader application of cost leadership or product differentiation may be better.

The potential for success using a cost leadership strategy or a product differentiation strategy might suggest that a firm can do even better by practicing both cost leadership and product differentiation. Porter advises against this, saying that firms that try to use both strategies risk being "stuck in the middle." A firm that tries to be a cost leader will typically try to take advantage of scale economies that favor volume over product features and attract customers who are sensitive to price. Product differentiation seeks to attract the less price sensitive customer who is willing to pay more, but the firm may need to spend more to create a product that does this. Firms that try to provide a good or service that costs less than the competition and yet is seen as better than the competition are endeavoring to achieve two somewhat opposing objectives at the same time.

CHAPTER 7

Firm Competition and Market Structure

Although highly competitive markets similar to the models in the previous chapter are desirable for an economy and occur for some goods and services, many important markets deviate significantly from the assumptions made in that discussion and operate differently. In this chapter we will consider some concepts and theories that help explain some of these other markets.

Why Perfect Competition Usually Does Not Happen

The perfect competition model (and its variants like monopolistic competition and contestable markets) represents an ideal operation of a market. As we noted in chapter 6, not only do the conditions of these models encourage aggressive competition that keeps prices as low as possible for buyers, but the resulting dynamics create the greatest value for all participants in the market in terms of surplus for consumers and producers.

Some markets resemble perfect competition more than others. Agricultural markets, particularly up through the beginning of the 20th century, were viewed as being close to a real-world version of a perfectly competitive market. There were many farmers and many consumers. No farmer and no consumer individually constituted sizeable fractions of the market activity, and both groups acted as price takers. With a modest amount of capital, one could acquire land, equipment, and seed or breeding stock to begin farming, especially when the United States was expanding and large volumes of unused land were available for purchase or homesteading. Although some farmers had better land and climate or were better suited for farming, the key information about how to farm was not impossible to learn.

However, in recent decades circumstances have changed, even for farming, in a way that deviates from the assumptions of perfect competition. Now farmers are unlikely to sell directly to consumers. Instead, they sell to food processing companies, large distributors, or grocery store chains that are not small and often not price takers. Many farming operations have changed from small, family-run businesses to large corporate enterprises. Even in markets where farming operations are still relatively small, the farmers form cooperatives that have market power. Additionally, the government takes an active role in the agriculture market with price supports and subsidies that alter farm production decisions.

One reason so few markets are perfectly competitive is that minimum efficient scales are so high that eventually the market can support only a few sellers. Although the contestable market model suggests that this factor alone does not preclude aggressive price competition between sellers, in most cases there is not really free entry for new firms. A new entrant will often face enormous startup capital requirements that prohibit entry by most modest-sized companies or individual entrepreneurs. Many markets are now influenced by brand recognition, so a new firm that lacks brand recognition faces the prospect of large promotional expenses and several periods with losses before being able to turn a profit. To justify the losses in the startup period, new entrants must expect they will see positive economic profits later to justify these losses, so the market is not likely to reach the stage of zero economic profit even if the new entrants join.

Due to economies of scope, few sellers offer just one product or are organized internally such that production of that one product is largely independent of the other products sold by that business. Consequently, it will be very difficult for a competitor, especially a new entrant in the market, to readily copy the breadth of operations of the most profitable sellers and immediately benefit from potential economies of scope.

Sellers that are vertically integrated may have control of upstream or downstream markets that make competition difficult for firms that focus on one stage in the value chain. For example, one firm may have control of key resources required in the production process, in terms of either the overall market supply or those resources of superior quality, making it hard for other firms to match their product in both cost and quality. Alternatively, a firm may control a downstream stage in the value chain, making it difficult for competitors to expand their sales, even if they price their products competitively.

As we will discuss in the next chapter, markets are subject to regulation by government and related public agencies. In the process of dealing with some perceived issues in these markets, these agencies will often block free entry of new firms and free exit of existing firms.

In our complex technological world, perfect information among all sellers and buyers is not always a reasonable assumption. Some sellers may possess special knowledge that is not readily known by their competition. Some producers may have protection of patents and exclusive rights to technology that gives them a sustained advantage that cannot be readily copied. On the buyer side, consumers usually have a limited perspective on the prices and products of all sellers and may not always pay the lowest price available for a good or service (although the Internet may be changing this to some degree).

Finally, for the perfect competition model to play out according to theory, there needs to be a reasonable level of stability so that there is sufficient time for the long-run consequences of perfect competition to occur. However, in our fast-changing world, the choices of goods and services available to consumers, the technologies for producing those products and services, and the costs involved in production are increasingly subject to rapid change. Before market forces can begin to gel to create price competition and firms can modify their operations to copy the most successful sellers, changes in circumstances may stir enough such that the market formation process starts anew.

Monopoly

Often, the main deterrent to a highly competitive market is market power possessed by sellers. In this section, we will consider the strongest form of seller market power, called a *monopoly*. In a monopoly there is only one seller, called a *monopolist*.

Recall that in perfect competition, each firm sees the demand curve it faces as a flat line, so it presumes it can sell as much as it wants, up to its production limit, at the prevailing market price. Even though the overall market demand curve decreases with increased sales volume, the single firm in perfect competition has a different perception because it is a small participant in the market and takes prices as given. In the case of flat demand curves, price and marginal revenue are the same, and since a profit-maximizing producer decides whether to increase or decrease production volume by comparing its marginal cost to marginal revenue, in this case the producer in perfect competition will sell more (if it has the capability) up the point where marginal cost equals price.

In a monopoly, the demand curve seen by the single selling firm is the entire market demand curve. If the market demand curve is downward sloping, the monopolist knows that marginal revenue will not equal price. As we discussed in chapter 2, when the demand curve is downward sloping, the marginal revenue corresponding to any quantity and price on the demand curve is less than the price (see Figure 7.1). Because the condition for optimal seller profit is where marginal revenue equals marginal cost, the monopolist will elect to operate at a quantity where those two quantities are in balance, which will be at volume marked Q_M in Figure 7.1.

Since the monopolist has complete control on sales, it will only sell at the quantity where marginal revenue equals marginal cost but will sell at the higher price associated with that quantity on the demand curve, P_M, rather than the marginal cost at a quantity of Q_M.

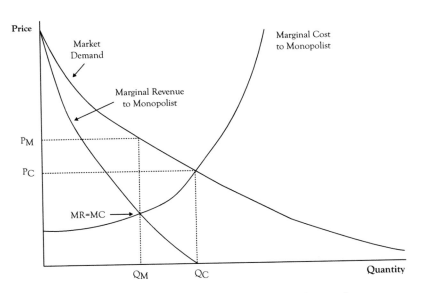

Figure 7.1. Graph showing the optimal quantity and price for a monopolist relative to the free market equilibrium price and quantity.

If the marginal cost curve for the monopolist were instead the combined marginal cost curves of small firms in perfect competition, the marginal cost curve would correspond to the market supply curve. The perfect competition market equilibrium would occur at a volume Q_C, with a price P_C. The monopolist could afford to function at this same volume and price and may even earn some economic profit. However, at this volume, marginal cost is greater than marginal revenue, indicating greater profit by operating at a lower volume at a higher price. The highest profit will result from selling Q_M units at a price of P_M. Unfortunately, consumers do worse at the monopolist's optimal operation as they pay a higher price and purchase fewer units. And as we noted in the previous chapter, the loss in consumer surplus will exceed the profit gain to the monopolist. This is the main reason monopolies are discouraged, if not outlawed, by governments.

Oligopoly and Cartels

Unless a monopoly is allowed to exist due to a government license or protection from a strong patent, markets have at least a few sellers. When a market has multiple sellers, at least some of which provide a significant portion of sales and recognize (like the monopolist) that their decisions on output volume will have an effect on market price, the arrangement is called an *oligopoly*.

At the extreme, sellers in an oligopoly could wield as much market power as a monopolist. This occurs in an oligopoly arrangement called a *cartel*, where the sellers coordinate their activities so well that they behave in effect like divisions of one enterprise, rather than as a competing business, that make independent decisions on quantity and price. (You may be familiar with the term cartel from the OPEC oil exporting group that is frequently described as a cartel. However, though OPEC has considerable market power and influence on prices, there are oil exporters that are not in OPEC, and internally OPEC only sets member targets rather than fully coordinating their operations.)

In theory, a cartel would operate at the same production volume and price as it would if its productive resources were all run by a monopolist. In a cartel, every member firm would sell at the same price and each firm would set its individual production volume such that every firm operates at the same marginal cost.

For the same reason that monopolies are considered harmful, cartels are usually not tolerated by governments for the regions in which those markets operate. Even the collusion that is a necessary component of a true cartel is illegal.

However, although cartels could theoretically function with the same power as a monopolist, if the cartel truly contains multiple members making independent decisions, there is a potential instability that can undo the cartel arrangement. Because monopolists gain added profit by reducing production volume and selling at a price above marginal cost, individual members may see an opportunity to defect, particularly if they can do so without being easily detected. Since the cartel price will be well above their marginal cost, they could profit individually by increasing their own production. Of course, if the defection is discovered and the other members retaliate by increasing their volumes as well, the result could be a substantially lower market price and lower economic profits for all cartel members.

Another problem for cartels is how to divide the profits. Suppose a cartel had two member firms, A and B. Firm A has more efficient facilities than Firm B, so the cartel solution will be to allow Firm A to provide the bulk of the production volume. However, if Firm A claims its share of the profits should be proportional to its share of the production volume, Firm B may object to voluntarily withholding its production only to allow to Firm A to grab most of the sales and profit, and the arrangement could end.

Also, since optimal cartel operation means that all firms set production so all have the same marginal cost, the firms need to share internal information for the cartel to determine the total volume where marginal revenue equals marginal cost and how that volume gets divided between firms. Again, some firms may have the incentive to keep the details of their operations private from other firms in the cartel.

Production Decisions in Noncartel Oligopolies

Oligopolies exist widely in modern economies. However, due to the reasons just cited, most do not function as cartels. Still, since these markets have relatively few sellers and each has a significant share of market sales, in many cases the total market production by oligopoly firms is less than would be expected if the market were perfectly competitive, and prices will be somewhat higher.

From the point of theory, the expected operation of the firm in perfect competition or in monopoly/cartel is straightforward. Assuming the firm in the perfect competition sufficiently understands its production costs, it will increase volume up to the point where its marginal cost exceeds the price. For a monopolist or cartel, production should increase up to point where marginal cost equals marginal revenue.

Oligopolies fall somewhere in between perfect competition and a cartel. However, the prescription of how to set optimal production volume is considerably more complex than either of the extremes. Like the monopolist, the oligopoly firm is aware that significant changes in its production level will have a significant effect on the market supply quantity, requiring a change in the market price to be in agreement with a downward sloping demand curve. However, while the firm is aware its production decisions will affect the market price, it is difficult to forecast the actual impact on price, even if the firm knows the behavior of the market demand curve.

A major reason for the complexity in determining the optimal production level is that the firm does not know how its oligopoly competitors will respond to its production decisions. For example, suppose a firm looks at the current market price and decides based on the market demand curve that it could increase its production volume by 1000 units per day and make a greater profit, even if the price dropped according to the market demand curve. Other sellers in the market will see the action taken and may decide that if the price is dropping and market demand is increasing that they could benefit by increasing their production to take advantage. As a consequence, the total market volume may increase more than expected, prices will drop more than expected, and the resulting gain in profit will be less than what the initial firm expected when it did its analysis.

Trying to figure out how to deal with reactions of other sellers not only is a vexing problem for sellers in oligopolies but has been a difficult challenge for academic economists who try to develop theories of oligopoly. The scholarly literature of economics is filled with elaborate mathematical models that attempt to address oligopoly operation. Next we will consider some of the insights of these analyses without the mathematics.

One approach that economists have used to model the behavior of oligopoly firms, known as the Bertrand model or price competition, is to assume all firms can anticipate the prices that will be charged by their competitors. If firms can reasonably anticipate the prices that other firms will charge and have a reasonable understanding of market demand, each firm can determine how customers would react to its own price and decide what production level and price leads to highest profit. The soft drink market is an example of a market that could operate in this manner.

Another approach for modeling oligopoly behavior, known as the Cournot model or quantity competition, is to assume all firms can determine the upcoming production levels or operating capacities of their competitors. For example, in the airline industry, schedules and gate arrangements are made months in advance. In essence, the airlines have committed to a schedule, their flying capacities are somewhat fixed, and what remains is to make the necessary adjustments to price to use the committed capacity effectively.

In comparing models where firms anticipate price to those where firms anticipate production volume or capacity commitment, firms that anticipate quantity levels tend to operate at lower production levels and charge higher prices. This occurs because in a quantity competition model, firms subtract the planned operation of their rivals from the market demand curve and assume the residual is the demand curve they will face. This leads to the presumption that the price elasticity of their own demand is the same as the price elasticity of overall market demand, whereas in price competition models the elasticity of the firm's own demand is seen as greater than the price elasticity of overall market demand (as was the case in the perfect competition model).

The number of selling firms also has an effect on the likely outcome of oligopoly competition. As the number of firms increases, the market equilibrium moves toward the equilibrium that would be expected in a perfectly competitive market of firms with the same aggregate production resources.

Another issue that can affect the prices and quantity volumes in an oligopoly market is the existence of a "leader" firm. A leader firm will make a decision on either its price or its volume/capacity commitment and then the remaining "follower" firms determine how they will react. An example of a leader firm in an industry might be Apple in the portable media player market. Apple decides on how it will price its iPod products and other manufacturers then decide how to price their products. Although the leader firm commits first in these models, in order to determine its own best course of action, it needs to anticipate how the follower firms will react to its decision.

Seller Concentration

Sellers in oligopolies can limit competition by driving out competitors, blocking entry by new competitors, or cooperating with other sellers with market power to keep prices higher than would be the case in a market with strong price competition. In order for sellers to exercise market power, either the market will have fairly few selling firms or there will be some selling firms that account for a large portion of all the market sales. When this happens, the market is said to have high seller concentration. Although high seller concentration in itself is not sufficient for exercise of seller power, it is generally a necessary condition and constitutes a potential for the exercise of seller power in the future. In this section, we will consider two numerical measures of market concentration: concentration ratios and the Herfindahl-Hirschmann Index (HHI).

Both measures of seller concentration are based on seller *market shares*. A firm's market share is the percentage of all market sales that are purchased from that firm. The highest possible market share is 100%, which is the market share of a monopolist. Market shares may be based either on the number of units sold or in terms of monetary value of sales. The latter use of monetary value is convenient when there are variations in the good or service sold and different prices are charged.

Concentration ratios are the result of sorting all sellers on the basis of market share, selecting a specified number of the firms with the highest market shares, and adding the market shares for those firms. For example, the concentration ratio CR_4 is the sum of the market shares for the four largest firms in terms of volume in a market and CR_8 is the sum of the eight largest firms in terms of volume. The U.S. Census Bureau periodically publishes concentration ratios for different industries in the United States.[1]

Suppose a market has 10 sellers with market shares (ranked from high to low) of 18%, 17%, 15%, 13%, 12%, 8%, 7%, 5%, 3%, and 2%. The CR_4 ratio for this market would be 63 (18 + 17 + 15 + 13), and the CR_8 ratio would be 95 (18 + 17 + 15 + 13 + 12 + 8 + 7 + 5).

Although concentration ratios are easy to calculate and easily understood, there are two shortcomings. First, the number of firms in the ratio is arbitrary. There is no reason that a four-firm concentration ratio indicates concentration potential any better than a three-firm or five-firm concentration ratio. Second, the ratio does not indicate whether there are one or two very large firms that clearly dominate all other firms in market share or the market shares for the firms included in the concentration ratio are about the same.

An alternative concentration measure that avoids these problems is the HHI. This index is computed by taking the market shares of all firms in the market, squaring the individual market shares, and finally summing them. The squaring has the effect of amplifying the larger market shares. The highest possible value of the HHI is 10,000, which occurs in the case of a monopoly ($10,000 = 100^2$). If, on the other hand, you had a market that had 100 firms that each had a market share of 1%, the HHI would be 100 ($1 = 1^2$, summed 100 times). For the previous 10-firm example, the HHI would be 1302. Although there is no inherent reason for squaring market shares, the HHI includes all firms in the computation (avoiding the issue of how many firms to include) and reflects the variation in magnitude of market shares.

As far as interpreting these concentration measures, the following statements provide some guidance on the potential for market power by sellers:

- If CR_4 is less than 40 or the HHI is less than 1000, the market has fairly low concentration and should be reasonably competitive.
- If CR_4 is between 40 and 60 or the HHI is between 1000 and 2000, there is a loose oligopoly that probably will not result in significant exercise of market power by sellers.
- If CR_4 is above 60 or the HHI is above 2000, then there is a tight oligopoly that has significant potential for exercise of seller power.
- If CR_1 is above 90 or the HHI is above 8000, one firm will be a clear leader and may function effectively as a monopoly.

Again, a high concentration measure indicates a potential for exploitation of seller power but not proof it will actually happen. Another important caution about these measures is that the scope of the market needs to be considered. In the case of banking services, even with the mergers that have resulted in higher seller concentration, if you look at measures of bank concentration at the national level, there seems be a loose oligopoly. However, if you limit the scope to banking in a single city or region, it is very likely that only few banks serve those areas. There can be modest concentrations when examining national markets but high concentration at the local level.

Competing in Tight Oligopolies: Pricing Strategies

In recent decades, economists have employed the applied mathematical tools of game theory to try to capture the dynamics of oligopoly markets. The initial research papers are generally abstract and very technical, but the acquired insights of some of this research have been presented in textbooks geared to nontechnical readers.[2] Game theory is outside the scope of this text, but we will consider some of the insights gained from the application of game theory in discussions about strategy in this and the following sections.

In this section, we will consider the economics underlying some of pricing strategies used by firms in monopolies and tight oligopolies.

1. *Deep discounting.* One exercise of seller power is to try to drive out existing competition. Deep discounting attempts to achieve this by setting the firm's price below cost, or at least below the average cost of a competitor. The intent is to attract customers from the competitor so that the competitor faces a dilemma of losses from either lost sales or being forced to follow suit and also set its price below cost. The firm initiating the deep discounting hopes that the competitor will decide that the best reaction is to exit the market. In a market with economies of scale, a large firm can better handle the lower price, and the technique may be especially effective in driving away a small competitor with a higher average cost. If and when the competitor is driven out of the market, the initiating firm will have a greater market share and increased market power that it can exploit in the form of higher prices and greater profits than before.

2. *Limit pricing.* A related technique for keeping out new firms is the technique of limit pricing. Again, the basic idea is to use a low price, but this time to ward off a new entrant rather than scare away an

existing competitor. Existing firms typically have lower costs than a new entrant will initially, particularly if there are economies of scale and high volume needed for minimum efficient scale. A limit price is enough for the existing firm to make a small profit, but a new entrant that needs to match the price to compete in the market will lose money. Again, when the new entrant is no longer a threat, the existing firm can reassert its seller power and raise prices for a sustained period well above average cost. As a game of strategy, the new entrant may reason that if it is willing to enter anyway and incur an initial loss, once its presence is in the market is established, the existing firm will realize their use of limit pricing did not work and decide it would be better to let prices go higher so that profits will increase, even if that allows the new entrant to be able to remain in the market.

3. *Yield management.* Another method for taking advantage of the power to set prices is yield management, where the firm abandons the practice of setting a fixed price and instead changes prices frequently. One goal is to try to extract higher prices from customers who are willing to pay more for a product or service. Normally, with a fixed announced price, customers who would have been willing to pay a significantly higher price get the consumer surplus. Even if the firm employs third-degree price discrimination and charges different prices to different market segments, some customers realize a surplus from a price well below the maximum they would pay. Using sophisticated software to continuously readjust prices, it is possible to capture higher prices from some of these customers. Yield management can also make it more difficult for other firms to compete on the basis of price since it does not have a known, fixed price to work against.

   A good example of yield management is the airline industry. Airlines have long employed price discrimination in forms of different classes of customers, different rates for flyers traveling over a weekend, and frequent flyer programs. However, in recent years, the price to buy a ticket can change daily, depending on the amount of time until the flight occurs and the degree to which the flight has already filled seats.

4. *Durable goods.* When firms in monopolies and oligopolies sell long-lived durable goods like cars and televisions, they have the option to sell to customers at different times and can attempt to do something similar to first-degree price discrimination by setting the price very

high at first. When the subset of customers who are willing to pay the most have made their purchase, the firms can drop the price somewhat and attract another tier of customers who are willing to pay slightly less than the first group. Progressively, the price will be dropped over time to attract most customers at a price close to the maximum they would be willing to pay.

However, economists have pointed out that customers may sense this strategy, and if patient, the customer can wait and pay a much lower price than the perceived value of the item. Even if the firm has little competition from other firms, a firm may find itself in the interesting situation of competing with itself in other production periods. In theoretical analyses of monopolies that sold durable goods, it has been demonstrated that when durable goods last a long time and customers are patient, even a monopolist can be driven to price items at marginal cost.[3]

One response to the durable goods dilemma is to sell goods with shorter product lives so that customers will need to return sooner to make a purchase. U.S. car manufacturers endeavored to do this in the middle of the 20th century but discovered that this opened the door for new entrants who sold cars that were designed to last longer.

Another response is to rent the use of the durable good rather than sell the good outright. This turns the good into a service that is sold for a specified period of time rather than a long-lived asset that is sold once to the customer (for at least a long time) and allows more standard oligopoly pricing that is applied for consumable goods and services. This arrangement is common with office equipment like copiers.

Competing in Tight Oligopolies: Nonpricing Strategies

Oligopoly firms also use a number of strategies that involve measures other than pricing to compete and maintain market power. Some of these strategies try to build barriers to entry by new entrants, whereas the intention of other measures is to distinguish the firm from other existing competitors.

1. *Advertising.* As we noted in chapter 3, most firms incur the expense of advertising. To some extent, advertising is probably necessary because

buyers, particularly household consumers, face a plethora of goods and services and realistically can actively consider only a limited subset of what is available. Advertising is a means of increasing the likelihood a firm's product or service is among those services actually considered.

When the firm is an upstream seller in a value chain with downstream markets, advertising may be directed at buyers in downstream markets. The intent is to encourage downstream buyers to look for products that incorporate the upstream firm's output. An example of such advertising is in pharmaceuticals, where drug manufacturers advertise in mass media with the intent of encouraging consumers to request a particular drug from their physicians.

In tight oligopolies, firms may boost the intensity of advertising well beyond the amount needed to inform buyers of the existence of their goods and services. Firms may advertise almost extravagantly with the idea of not only establishing brand recognition but making strong brand recognition essential to successful competition in the market. Once strong brand recognition takes hold in the market, new firms will need to spend much more to establish brand recognition than existing firms spend to maintain brand recognition. Hence new entrants are discouraged by what is perceived as a high startup fee, which is a type of barrier to entry.

2. *Excess capacity.* Ordinarily a firm will plan for a capacity that is sufficient to support the production volume. Because capacity is often planned in advance and actual production volume may vary from period to period, the firm may have some excess capacity in some periods. And since there is inherent uncertainty in future demand, firms may even invest in capacity that is never fully utilized.

However, firms in oligopolies may invest, or partially invest, in capacity well beyond what is needed to cover fluctuations in volume and accommodation of uncertainty as a means of competing. If the sellers in an oligopoly have been successful in collectively holding back on quantity to drive up the price and profits, since the price is well above average cost, there is an opportunity for one firm to offer the product at a lower price, attract a sizeable fraction of the new customers attracted by the lower price, and make a sizeable individual gain in profit. This gambit may come from a new entrant or even an existing seller. This tactic may work, at least for a time, if the firm introducing the lower price does it by surprise and the other firms are not prepared to ramp up production rapidly to match the initiator's move.

One way to protect against an attack of this nature is to have a significant amount of excess capacity, or at least some additional capacity that could be upgraded and brought online quickly. The firm doing this may even want to clearly reveal this to other sellers or potential sellers as a signal that if another firm were to try an attack of this nature, they are prepared to respond quickly and make sure they take advantage of the increased sales volume.

3. *Reputation and warranties.* As a result of fluctuations in cost or buyer demand, being a seller in a market may be more attractive in some periods than others. During periods that are lucrative for being a seller, some firms may be enticed to enter on a short-term basis, with minimal long-term commitments, enjoy a portion of the spoils of the favorable market, and then withdraw when demand declines or costs increase.

Firms that intend to remain in the market on an ongoing basis would prefer that these hit-and-run entrants not take away a share of the profits when the market is attractive. One measure to discourage this is to make an ongoing presence desired by the customer so as to distinguish the product of the ongoing firms from the product of the short-term sellers. As part of advertising, these firms may emphasize the importance of a firm's reputation in providing a quality product that the firm will stand behind.

Another measure is to make warranties a part of the product, a feature that is only of value to the buyer if the seller is likely to be available when a warranty claim is made. Like high-cost advertising, even the scope of the warranty may become a means of competition, as is seen in the automobile industry where warranties may vary in time duration, number of driven miles, and systems covered.

4. *Product bundling.* In chapter 3, we discussed the notion of complementary goods and services. This is a relationship in which purchasers of one good or service become more likely to purchase another good or service. Firms may take advantage of complementary relationships by selling products together in a bundle, where consumers have the option to purchase multiple products as a single item at lower total cost than if the items were purchased separately. This can be particularly effective if there are natural production

economies of scope in these complementary goods. If competitors are unable to readily match the bundled product, the firm's gain can be substantial.

A good example of successful product bundling is Microsoft Office. Microsoft had developed the word processing software Word, the spreadsheet software Excel, the presentation software PowerPoint, and the database software Access. Individually, each of these products was clearly outsold by other products in those specialized markets. For example, the favored spreadsheet software in the late 1980s was Lotus 1-2-3. When Microsoft decided to bundle the packages and sell them for a modest amount more than the price of a single software package, customers perceived a gain in value, even if they did not actively use some of the packages. Since all the components were software and distributed on floppy disks (and later on CDs and via web downloads), there was a strong economy of scope. However, when Microsoft introduced the bundle, the firms selling the leader products in the individual markets were not able to match the product bundling, even though some attempted to do so after Microsoft has usurped the market. Consequently, not only was the product bundle a success, but the individual components of Microsoft Office each became the dominant products.

5. *Network effects and standards.* In some markets, the value of a product to a buyer may be affected by the number of other buyers of the product. For example, a cell phone becomes more valuable if most of the people you would like to phone quickly also carry a cell phone. Products that increase in value when the adoption rate of the product increases, even if some units are sold by competitors, are said to have "network effects."

One impact of network effects is that industry standards become important. Often network effects occur because the products purchased need to use compatible technologies with other products. In some markets, this may result in some level of cooperation between firms, such as when appliance manufacturers agree to sell units with similar dimensions or connections.

However, sometimes multiple standards emerge and firms may select to support one standard as a means of competing against a firm that uses another standard. Sellers may group into alliances to help improve their success via network effects. In the once-vibrant market for VCR tapes and tape players, the initial standard for producing tapes was called Betamax. This Betamax standard was developed by Sony and used in the VCR players that Sony produced. Soon after Betamax was introduced, the electronics manufacturer JVC introduced the VHS standard. Consumers first had to purchase the VCR player, but the value of the product was affected by the availability and variety of tapes they could acquire afterward, which was determined by whether their player used the Betamax standard or the VHS standard. Eventually the VHS standard prevailed, favoring JVC and the other firms that allied with JVC.

Up until the videotape was eclipsed by the DVD, the VCR industry moved to using the VHS standard almost exclusively. This illustrates a frequent development in a market with strong network effects: a winner-take-all contest. Another example of a winner-take-all situation can be seen with operating systems in personal computers. Although there were multiple operating systems available for PCs in the 1980s, eventually Microsoft's MS-DOS and later Windows operating systems achieved a near monopoly in personal computer operating systems. Again, the driver is network effects. Companies that produced software saw different markets depending on the operating system used by the buyer. As MS-DOS/Windows increased its market share, companies were almost certain to sell a version of their product for this operating system, usually as their first version and perhaps as their only version. This, in turn, solidified Microsoft's near monopoly. Although other operating systems still exist and the free operating system Linux and the Apple Macintosh OS have succeeded in some niches, Microsoft Windows remains the dominant operating system.

Buyer Power

The bulk of this chapter looked at facets of market power that is possessed and exploited by sellers. However, in markets with a few buyers that individually make a sizeable fraction of total market purchases, buyers can exercise power that will influence the market price and quantity.

The most extreme form of buyer power is when there is a single buyer, called a *monopsony*. If there is no market power among the sellers, the buyer is in a position to push the price down to the minimum amount needed to induce a seller to produce the last unit. The supply curve for seller designates this price for any given level of quantity. Although the monopsonist could justify purchasing additional units up to the point where the supply curve crosses its demand curve, the monopsonist can usually get a higher value by purchasing a smaller amount at a lower price at another point on the supply curve.

Assuming the monopsonist is not able to discriminate in its purchases and buy each unit at the actual marginal cost of the unit, rather buying all units at the marginal cost of the last unit acquired, the monopsonist is aware that when it agrees to pay a slightly higher price to purchase an additional unit, the new price will apply to all units purchased. As such, the marginal cost of increasing its consumption will be higher than the price charged for an additional unit. The monopsonist will maximize its value gained from the purchases (amount paid plus consumer surplus) at the point where the marginal cost of added consumption equals the marginal value of that additional unit, as reflected in its demand curve. This optimal solution is depicted in Figure 7.2, with the quantity Q_S being the amount it will purchase and price P_S being the price it can impose on the sellers. Note, as with the solution with a seller monopoly, the quantity is less than would occur if the market demand curve were the composite of small buyers with no market power. However, the monopsonist price is less than the monopoly price because the monopsonist can force the price down to the supply curve rather than to what a unit is worth on the demand curve.

When there are multiple large buyers, there will be increased competition that will generally result in movement along the supply curve toward the point where it crosses the market demand curve. However, unless these buyers are aggressively competitive, they are likely to pay less than under the perfect competition solution by either cooperating with other buyers to keep prices low or taking other actions intended to keep the other buyers out of the market.

An example of a monopsonist would be an employer in a small town with a single large business, like a mining company in a mountain community. The sellers in this case are the laborers. If laborers have only one place to sell their labor in the community, the employer possesses significant market power that it can use to drive down wages and even change the nature of the service provided by demanding more tiring or dangerous working conditions. When the industrial revolution created strong

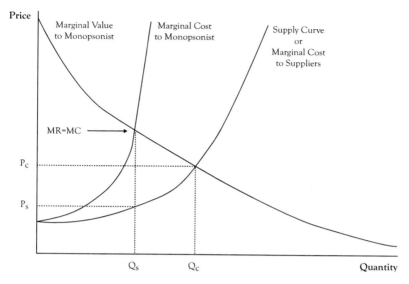

Figure 7.2. Graph showing the optimal quantity and price for a monopsonist relative to the free market equilibrium price and quantity.

economies of scale that supported very large firms with strong employer purchasing power, laborers faced a difficult situation of low pay and poor working conditions. One of the reasons for the rise of the labor unions in the United States was as a way of creating power for the laborers by requiring a single transaction between the employer and all laborers represented by the union.

CHAPTER 8

Market Regulation

In the previous chapter, we recognized the possibility that markets left to their own devices may not result in the best outcomes when viewed from the perspective of the net impact on all participants in the market. In some cases, the difference between an unregulated market and what might be possible with some outside influence invites the consideration of measures that might be taken by a government or other monitoring agency. In this final chapter, we will examine some of the key categories where intervention may be considered and what regulatory measures can be taken.

Free Market Economies Versus Collectivist Economies

The well-being and stability of any society depends on whether the members of that society are able to acquire the goods and services they need or want. In primitive societies, these issues were settled by either a recognized authority figure (e.g., a king or military leader) or use of force. In modern times, even though we still have kings and dictators, the source of authority is likely to be government laws and agencies. Societies that primarily use centralized authorities to manage the creation and distribution of goods and services are called collectivist economies. The philosophy of communism is based on the prescription that centralized authority is the best means of meeting the needs and wants of its citizens.

For millennia, even collectivist societies have included some level of commerce in the form of trade or purchases with currency. The use of the word "market" to describe the activities of buyers and sellers for goods and services derives from town gathering areas where such exchanges took place. Early markets were limited in terms of how much of the total goods and services in a society were negotiated, but in recent centuries, markets took an increasing role in the allocation of goods and services, starting in Europe. Today, most developed countries operate in a manner where exchange by markets is the rule rather than the exception. Societies that rely primarily on markets to determine the creation of goods and services are called free market economies.

Countries will lean toward being either more free market based or more collectivist, but no country is purely one or the other. In the United States, which is predominantly a free market economy, some services, like fire protection, are provided by public authorities. In China, which is a communist nation, free market activity has thrived in recent decades. As we will discuss in this chapter, even when markets are the main vehicle for allocation, there is some degree of regulation on their operation.

Efficiency and Equity

There is a subfield of economics called "welfare economics" that focuses on evaluating the performance of markets. Two of the criteria used to assess markets are efficiency and equity.

Efficiency is a shortened reference to what economists call *Pareto efficiency*. The outcome of a set of exchanges between decision-making units in a market or network of markets is called *Pareto efficient* if it would be impossible to modify how the exchanges occurred to make one party better off without making another party decidedly worse off. If there is a way to change the exchanges or conditions of the exchanges so that every party is at least as satisfied and there is at least one party that is more satisfied, the existing collection of exchanges is not Pareto efficient.

Pure Pareto efficiency is an ideal rather than a condition that is possible in the complex world in which we live. Still, in clear cases where some intervention in the market can result in significant overall improvement in the pattern of exchanges, regulation merits consideration.

One circumstance where this notion of efficiency is not fulfilled is when there is waste of resources that could have some productive value. When markets leave the useful resources stranded to spoil or be underutilized, there is probably a way to reconfigure exchanges to create improvement for some and at a loss to no one.

In the case of monopoly, which we examined in chapter 7, the price and quantity selected by the monopolist is not efficient because it would be possible, at least in principle, to require the monopolist to set the price at the perfect competition equilibrium, reclaim the deadweight loss in consumer surplus and producer surplus, and redistribute enough of the surplus so the monopolist is as well off as it was at the monopoly price and the consumers are better off.

Equity corresponds to the issue of whether the distribution of goods and services to individuals and the profits to firms are fair. Unfortunately, there is no simple single principle, like Pareto efficiency, that has been adopted as the primary standard for equity. Although there is general support for the idea that the distribution of goods and services ought to favor those with greater talents or those who work harder, there are also those who view access to basic goods and services as reasonable expectations of all citizens. Despite the impossibility of developing a general consensus on what constitutes equity, when enough people become concerned that the distribution of goods and services is too inequitable, there are likely to be pressures on those in political power or political unrest.

Most microeconomists tend to view active regulation of individual markets as worthy of consideration when there are inefficiencies in the functioning of those markets. Since managerial economics (and this text) has a microeconomics focus, we will address the merit of market regulation from this perspective as well.

Problems of inequity are usually regarded as a problem of macroeconomics, best handled by wealth transfers, such as income taxes and welfare payments rather than intervention in the markets for goods and services. Still, there are instances where regulatory actions directed at specific markets reflect equity concerns, such as requiring companies to offer basic services at lifeline rates for low-income customers.

Circumstances in Which Market Regulation May Be Desirable

When a market operates inefficiently, economists call the situation a *market failure*. In this chapter, we will address the generic types of market failure:

- Market failure caused by seller or buyer concentration
- Market failure that occurs when parties other than buyers and sellers are affected by market transactions but do not participate in negotiating the transaction

- Market failure that occurs because an actual market will not emerge or cannot sustain operation due to the presence of free riders who benefit from, but do not bear the full costs of, market exchanges
- Market failure caused by poor seller or buyer decisions, due to a lack of sufficient information or understanding about the product or service

In all four situations, the case can be made that a significant degree of inefficiency results when the market is left to proceed without regulation.

Economists are fond of repeating the maxim "There is no free lunch." Regulation is not free and is difficult to apply correctly. Regulation can create unexpected or undesirable effects in itself. At the conclusion of the chapter, we will consider some of the limitations of regulation.

Regulation to Offset Market Power of Sellers or Buyers

In chapter 7, we considered how monopolies and monopsonies would try to force changes in the price and quantity to move the market to their advantage, but at an even greater cost to the other side of the market. Again, this is not simply an equity concern that one party is getting most of the surplus created by the market (although that may be a legitimate concern) but rather the exertion of market power results in a net loss in total social surplus.

Seller competition is not only helpful in lowering prices and increasing volume and consumer surplus, but firms also compete in terms of product differentiation. When a monopoly or oligopoly emerges and the seller(s) have a sustainable arrangement that generates economic profits, the firms do not have the incentive to spend money in developing better products. The stagnation of the product sold represents another loss in potential value to the consumer.

Unfortunately, monopolies or tight oligopolies can readily develop in markets, especially when there are strong economies of scale and market power effects. For this reason, there are general antitrust laws that empower governments to prevent the emergence of monopolies and tight oligopolies. Some of these laws and regulations actually cite measures of market concentration that can be used as a basis for opposing any buyouts or mergers that will increase market concentration. Where market concentration has already advanced to high levels, firms can be instructed to break up into separate companies. About a century ago, monopolies had developed in important U.S. industries like petroleum, railroads, and electric power. Eventually, the U.S. federal government mandated these monopolies split apart.

As mentioned in earlier chapters, the fact that there are a few large sellers does not automatically constitute abusive use of market power if there is free entry and active competition between sellers. However, if those large sellers collude to hold back production volumes and raise prices, there is a loss in market surplus. The United States has laws that outlaw such collusion. While firms may be able to collude with indirect signals that are difficult for government antitrust units to identify at the time, courts will consider testimony that demonstrates that collusion has taken place.

In chapter 7, we discussed the market power tactics of using low prices to drive out existing competitors and keep out new entrants. When the purpose of the price drop is merely to chase out competition, the practice is labeled predatory pricing and is considered illegal. Of course, the firms engaging in price decreases often take the position that they are in a competitive market and are simply competing on the basis of reduced profit margins, just as firms are expected to compete according to the theory of the perfect competition model. Courts are left to determine whether such actions are simply aggressive competition or are intended to create a more concentrated market that allows for greater profits in the long run.

As an alternative to taking actions to limit large firms from exploiting their size, another form of regulation is to encourage more competition by helping small or new competitors. Either subsidies or tax breaks may be offered to help these firms offset the disadvantages of being small in the market and to eventually emerge as an independent player in the market.

In cases where a concentrated seller market exists and the product or service is considered critical to the buyers and the overall economy, the government may decide to intervene strongly by setting a limit on prices or mandating that the product be provided at a minimum quantity and quality.

In situations where there is buyer power, the goal of regulation may be to push prices higher. For example, in agriculture crop markets where the seller farmers often have little market power, but there is concentration on the buyer side, the government will try to keep prices higher by mandating minimum prices or direct assistance to farmers in the form of price support programs.

Another response to market power on one side of the market is to support market power on the other side of the market. Using the crop market example again where there is buyer power, the government has sanctioned the creation of grower cooperatives that control the quantity of the amount sold to processors and thus keep the price higher.

Natural Monopoly

In industries where the minimum efficient scale is very high, it may be that the lowest average cost is achieved if there is only one seller providing all the goods or services. Examples of such a service might be transmission and distribution of electric power or telephone service. This situation often occurs when total costs are very high but marginal costs are low. Economists call such markets *natural monopolies*.

Unfortunately, if just one firm is allowed to serve the entire market, the firm will be tempted to exploit the monopoly position rather than pass its lower cost in the form of lower prices. One response to this situation is to conclude that the service should be provided by a public agency rather than a private company. In the case of telephone service, European countries often run the telephone system rather than a corporation like AT&T.

Another response is to go ahead and allow the private firm to be the sole seller but require regulatory approval for the prices to be charged. These regulated monopolies are often called public utilities, even though the operator may be a private corporation. In principle, this regulated monopoly could achieve the best of both worlds, letting a private company serve the market, while making sure the buyer is enjoying the benefits of the low average cost. In fact, this notion of a regulated monopoly was first proposed by AT&T when it feared that its near monopoly would be usurped by the government. Governments create agencies like state public utility commissions to review cost information with the public utility corporation in deciding on the prices or service rates that will be approved.

A potential concern when a single provider is allowed to operate as a regulated monopoly is that, without competition, the provider has little incentive for innovation or cost cutting. This could be the case whether the provider operated as a government agency or a public utility corporation. When a public utility corporation understands that it will be reimbursed for its costs plus an amount to cover the opportunity costs of assets or capital contributed by the corporation's owners, the challenge is to be able to justify the costs rather than seek to trim its costs. Some regulatory agencies try to motivate regulated monopolies to be innovative or cut costs by allowing them to keep some of the surplus created in exchange for lower rates in the future. However, regulation is a game where the regulatory agency and the public utility corporation are both competing and cooperating. And the transaction costs of outside oversight of the regulatory monopoly are substantial. So, as noted earlier, there is no free lunch.

Externalities

The second generic type of market failure is when parties other than the buyer and seller are significantly affected by the exchange between the buyer and seller. However, these other parties do not participate in the negotiation of the sale. Consequently, the quantities sold and prices charged do not reflect the impacts on these parties.

Economists call the effects of market activity on the third parties *externalities* because they fall outside the considerations of buyer and seller. Although the concern with significant externalities is usually due to harm to the third party, externalities can be beneficial to third parties as well. Harmful externalities are called *negative externalities*; beneficial externalities are called *positive externalities*.

Some examples of negative externalities are pollution of air or water that is experienced by persons other than those directly related to the seller or buyer, injury or death to another person resulting from the market exchange, inconvenience and annoyances caused by loud noise or congestion, and spoiling of natural habitats. Some examples of positive externalities are spillover effects of research and development used for one product to other products or other firms, training of a worker by one firm and thereby creating a more valuable worker for a future employer, stimulation of additional economic activity outside the market, and outside benefactors of problem-solving services like pest control.

Negative externalities clearly create an inequity because the third parties are harmed without any compensation. However, significant negative externalities also create inefficiency. Recall that inefficiency means there is a way to make someone better off and no one worse off. Take the case of a negative externality like air pollution caused when an automobile owner purchases gasoline to use in his car. Hypothetically, if a representative for outside parties were present at the negotiation for the sale, she might be willing to pay an amount to the buyer and an amount to the seller in exchange for foregoing the sale by compensating the buyer with the consumer surplus they would have received and the producer with the economic profit they would have received, with the sum of those payments being worth the avoidance of the externality impact of the air pollution.

Even in the case of a positive externality, there is inefficiency. However, in this case, the third parties would actually benefit from more market exchanges than the sellers and buyers would be willing to transact. In principle, if third parties could participate in the market, they would be willing to pay the buyer or seller up to the value of the positive externality if it would induce more market activity.

Regulation of externalities usually takes two forms: legal and economic. Legal measures are sanctions that forbid market activity, restrict the volume of activity, or restrict those who are allowed to participate as buyers and sellers. As examples of these, if an appliance is prone to start fires that might burn an entire apartment complex and injure others besides the buyer, the sale of the appliance might be banned outright. If sales of water drawn from a river would threaten a wildlife habit, sales may be limited to a maximum amount. A firearms manufacturer might be allowed to sell firearms but would be restricted to sell only to people of at least a certain age who do not have a criminal record. Because legal measures require monitoring and enforcement by the government, there are transaction costs. When a legal measure is excessive, it may actually create a reverse form of inefficiency from denying surplus value to buyers and sellers that exceeds the benefit to other parties.

Externality Taxes

The most practiced economic instrument to address market externality is a tax. Those who purchase gasoline are likely to pay the sum of the price required by the gasoline station owner to cover his costs (and any economic profit he has the power to generate) plus a tax on each unit of gasoline that covers the externality cost of gasoline consumption such as air pollution, wear and tear on existing public roads, needs for expanding public roads to support more driving, and policing of roads.

Theoretically, there is an optimal level for setting a tax. The optimum tax is the value of the marginal externality damage created by consumption of an additional item from a market exchange. If each gallon of gasoline causes $1.50 worth of externality damage, that would be the correct tax.

In the case of positive externalities, the optimum tax is negative. In other words, the government actually pays the seller an amount per unit in exchange for a reduction of an equal amount in the price. Theoretically, the optimum tax would be the negative of the marginal value of a unit of consumption to third parties. For example, if the positive externality from hiring an unemployed person and giving that person employment skills would be worth $2.00 per hour, the employer could be subsidized $2.00 per hour to make it more attractive for them to hire that kind of person.

Although the notion of an externality tax sounds straightforward, actual implementation is difficult. Even when there is general agreement that a significant externality exists, placing a dollar value on that externality can be extremely difficult and controversial. The optimal tax is the marginal impact on third parties; however, there is no guarantee that the total tax collected in this fashion will be the total amount needed to compensate for the total externality impact. The total collected may be either too little or too much.

Also, recall the impact of a tax from the earlier discussion of comparative statics in competitive markets in chapter 6. A tax has the impact of either raising the supply curve upward (if the seller pays the tax) or moving the demand curve downward (if the buyer pays the tax). See Figure 8.1 for a graphic illustration of a tax charged to the buyer. To the extent that the supply and demand curves are price elastic, the tax will lower

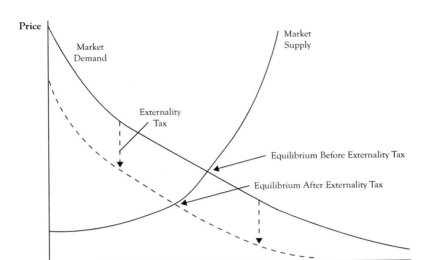

Figure 8.1. Change in market equilibrium in response to imposing an externality tax. Note the tax may cause a decrease in the equilibrium quantity, which may change the optimal externality tax.

the amount consumed, thereby diminishing the externality somewhat and possibly changing the marginal externality cost. Consequently, actual externality taxes require considerable public transaction costs and may not be at the correct level for the best improvement of market efficiency.

Regulation of Externalities Through Property Rights

The economist Ronald Coase, whom we mentioned earlier in the context of the optimal boundaries of the firm and transaction costs, postulated that the problem of externalities is really a problem of unclear or inadequate property rights.[1] If the imposition of negative externalities were considered to be a right owned by a firm, the firm would have the option to resell those rights to another firm that was willing to pay more than the original owner of the right would appreciate by keeping and exercising the privilege.

For those externalities that society is willing to tolerate at some level because the externality effects either are acceptable if limited (e.g., the extraction of water from rivers) or come from consumption that society does not have a sufficiently available alternative (e.g., air pollution caused by burning coal to generate electricity), the government representatives can decide how much of the externality to allow and who should get the initial rights. The initial rights might go to existing sellers in the markets currently creating the externalities or be sold by the government in an auction.

An example of this form of economic regulation is the use of "cap and trade" programs designed to limit greenhouse gas emissions. In cases where this has been implemented, new markets emerge for trading the rights. If the right is worth more to another firm than to the owner, the opportunity cost of retaining that right to the current owner will be high enough to justify selling some of those rights on the emissions market. If the opportunity cost is sufficiently high, the owner may decide to sell all its emissions rights and either shut down its operations or switch to a technology that generates no greenhouse gases.

If the value of emissions rights to any firm is less than the externality cost incurred if the right is exercised, the public can also purchase those externality rights and either retire them permanently or hold them until a buyer comes along that is willing to pay at least as much as the impact of the externality cost to parties outside the market exchange.

High Cost to Initial Entrant and the Risk of Free Rider Producers

Next, we will consider the third generic type of market failure, or the inability for a market to form or sustain operation due to free riders, by looking at two causes of this kind of failure in this section and the next section. Although the sources are different, both involve a situation where some party benefits from the market exchange without incurring the same cost as other sellers or buyers.

New products and services are expensive for the first firm to bring them to market. There may be initial failures in the development of a commercial product that add to the cost. The firm will start very high on the learning curve because there is no other firm to copy or hire away its talent. The nature of buyer demand for the product is uncertain, and the seller is likely to overcharge, undercharge, or alternatively set initial production targets that are too high or too low.

If the firm succeeds, it may initially have a monopoly, but unless there are barriers of entry, new entrant firms will be attracted by the potential profits. These firms will be able to enter the market with less uncertainty about how to make the product commercially viable and the nature of demand for the product. And these firms may be able to determine how the initial entrant solved the problems of designing the product or service and copy the process at far less initial cost than was borne by the initial entrant.

If the product sold by the initial firm and firms that enter the market later look equivalent to the buyer, the buyer will not pay one of these firms more than another just based on its higher cost. If the market becomes competitive for sellers, the price is likely to be driven by the marginal cost. New entrant firms may do well, but the initial entrant firm is not likely to get a sufficient return on the productive assets it had invested from startup. In effect, the other firms would be *free riders* that benefit from the startup costs of the initial entrant without having to contribute to that cost.

The market failure occurs here because, prior to even commencing with a startup, the would-be initial entrant may look ahead, see the potential for free riders and the inability to generate sufficient profits to justify the startup costs, and decide to scrap the idea. This market failure is a market inefficiency because it is hypothetically possible for the initial entrant, subsequent entrants, and buyers to sit at a negotiation and reach an arrangement where startup costs are shared by the firms or buyer prices are set higher to cover the startup costs, so that all firms and buyers decide they would be better off with that negotiated arrangement than if the market never materialized. Unfortunately, such negotiations are unlikely to emerge from the unregulated activities of individual sellers and buyers.

One of the main regulatory measures to address this problem is to guarantee the initial entrant a high enough price and sufficient volume of sales to justify the up-front investment. Patents are a means by which a product or service that incorporates a new idea or process gives the developer a monopoly, at least for production that uses that process or idea, for a certain period of time. Patents are an important element in the pharmaceutical industry in motivating the development of new drugs because there is a long period of development and testing and a high rate of failure. Companies selling patent-protected drugs will sell those products at monopoly prices. However, the process for manufacturing the drug is usually readily reproducible by other companies, even small "generic" manufacturers, so the price of the drug will drop precipitously when patent protection expires. In fact, patent-holding firms will usually drop the price shortly prior to patent expiration in an attempt to extract sales from the lower portion of the demand curve before other firms can enter.

In cases where there is not a patentable process, but nonetheless a high risk of market failure due to frightening away the initial entrant, government authorities may decide to give exclusive operating rights for at least a period of time. This tool was used to encourage the expansion of cable television to the initial entrant in a region to justify the high up-front expenses.

Other government interventions can be the provision of subsidies to the initial entrant to get them to market a new product. The government may decide to fund the up-front research and development and then make the acquired knowledge available to any firm that enters the market so there is not such a difference between being the initial entrant or a subsequent entrant. Another option is for the government itself to serve in the role of the initial entrant and then, when the commercial viability is demonstrated, privatize the product or service.

Public Goods and the Risk of Free Rider Consumers

Most goods and services that are purchased are such that one person or a very limited group of persons can enjoy the consumption of the good or, for a durable good, the use of that good at a specific time. For example, if a consumer purchases an ice cream bar, she can have the pleasure of eating the ice cream bar or share it with perhaps one or two other people at most. A television set can only be in one home at any given time. Economists call such products *rival goods*.

In the case of rival goods, the party consuming the product is easily linked to the party that will purchase the product. Whether the party purchases the product depends on whether the value obtained is at least as high as the price.

However, there are other goods that are largely nonrival. This means that several people might benefit from an item produced and sold in the market without diminishing the benefit to others, especially the party that actually made the purchase. For example, if a homeowner pays for eradication of mosquitoes around his house, he likely will exterminate mosquitoes that would have affected his neighbors. The benefit obtained by the neighbors does not detract from the benefit gained by the buyer. When benefits of a purchased good or service can benefit others without detracting from the party making the purchase, economists call the product a *public good*.[2]

The difficulty with public goods is that the cost to create a public good by a seller may be substantially more than an individual buyer is willing to pay but less than the collective value to all who would benefit from the purchase. For example, take the cost of tracking down criminals. An individual citizen may benefit from the effort to locate and arrest a criminal, but the individual is not able or willing to hire a police force of the scale needed to conduct such operations. Even though the result of hiring a police force may be worth more to all citizens who benefit than what a company would charge to do it, since there are no individual buyers, the market will not be able to function and there is market failure.

As with the market failure for initial entrants with high startup cost, there is a potential agreement where all benefactors would be willing to pay an amount corresponding to their value that, if collected, would cover the cost of creating the good or service. The problem is that individuals would prefer to let someone else pay for it and be a free rider. So the inability of the market to function is a case of inefficiency.

In perfect competition, the optimal price to be charged is the marginal cost of serving another customer. However, in the case of public goods, the marginal cost of serving an additional benefactor can be essentially zero. This creates an interesting dilemma whereby the theoretical optimal pricing for the good is to charge a price of zero. Of course, that adds to the market failure problem because the cost of production of the good or service is not zero, so it is not feasible to operate a market of private sellers and buyers in this manner.

Usually the only way to deal with a public good of sufficient value is for the government to provide the good or service or pay a private organization to run the operation without charging users, or at least not fully charging users. This is how key services like the military, police protection, fire stations, and public roadways are handled. There may be some ability to charge users a modest fee for some services, but the revenue would not be sufficient to support a market served by private firms. For example, governments build dams as a means of flood control, irrigation, and water recreation. The agency that manages the dam may charge entry fees for boating on the lake or use of water released from the dam. However, the agency still needs to remain a public agency and likely needs additional finances from other public revenues like income or sales taxes to support its continued operations.

An interesting public good problem has emerged with the ability to make high-quality digital copies of books and music at very low marginal cost. When someone purchases a music CD (or downloads a file of commercial music) and then allows a copy to be made for someone else, the creation of the copy does not diminish the ability to enjoy the music by the person who made the initial purchase. Artists and producers claim that the recipients of the copies are enjoying the media products as free riders and denying the creators of the products full payment from all who enjoy their products, although there is some debate whether copying is a bona fide market failure concern.[3] Nonetheless, publishers have pursued measures to discourage unauthorized copies, whether via legal prohibition or technology built into the media, or media players, to thwart the ability to make a clean copy.

Market Failure Caused by Imperfect Information

In the earlier discussion of the perfect competition model, we noted the assumption of perfect information of buyers and sellers. Theoretically, this means that buyers and sellers not only know the full array of prices being charged for goods and services, but they also know the production capabilities of sellers and the utility preferences of buyers. As part of that discussion, we noted that this assumption is not fully satisfied in real markets, yet sellers and buyers may have a reasonably complete understanding of market conditions, particularly within the limits of the types of products and geographic areas in which they normally participate.

Imperfect information can be due to ignorance or uncertainty. If the market participant is aware that better information is available, information becomes another need or want. Information may be acquired through an economic transaction and becomes a commodity that is a cost to the buyer or seller. Useful information is available as a market product in forms like books, media broadcasts, and consulting services.

In some cases, uncertainty can be transferred to another party as an economic exchange. Insurance is an example of product where the insurance company assumes the risk of defined uncertain outcomes for a fee.

Still, there remain circumstances where ignorance or risk is of considerable consequence and cannot be addressed by an economic transaction. One such instance is where one party in an economic exchange deliberately exploits the ignorance of another party in the transaction to its own advantage and to the disadvantage of the unknowing party. This type of situation is called a *moral hazard*. For example, if an entrepreneur is raising capital from outside investors, he may present a biased view of the prospects of the firm that only includes the good side of the venture to attract the capital, but the outside investors eventually lose their money due to potentially knowable problems that would have discouraged their investment if those problems had been known.

In some cases, the missing information is not technically hidden from the party, but the effective communication of the key information does not occur. For example, a consumer might decide to acquire a credit card from a financial institution and fail to note late payment provisions in the fine print that later become a negative surprise. Whether such communication constitutes proper disclosure or moral hazard is debatable, but the consequences of the bad decision occur nonetheless.

Exchanges with moral hazard create equity and efficiency concerns. If one party is taking advantage of another party's ignorance, there is an arguable equity issue. However, the inadequate disclosure results in a market failure when the negative consequences to the ignorant party more than offset the gains to the parties that disguise key information. This is an inefficient market because the losing parties could compensate the other party for its gains and still suffer less than they did from the incidence of moral hazard.

Further, the impact of poor information may spread beyond the party that makes a poor decision out of ignorance. As we have seen with the financial transactions in mortgage financing in the first decade of this century, the consequences of moral hazard can be deep and widespread, resulting in a negative externality as well.

Market failures from imperfect information can occur even when there is no intended moral hazard. In chapter 5, we discussed the concept of adverse selection, where inherent risk from uncertainty about the other party in an exchange causes a buyer or seller to assume a pessimistic outcome as a way of playing it safe and minimizing the consequences of risk. However, a consequence of playing it safe is that parties may decide to avoid agreements that actually could work. For example, a company might consider offering health insurance to individuals. An analysis might indicate that such insurance is feasible based on average incidences of medical claims and willingness of individuals to pay premiums. However, due to the risk that the insurance policies will be most attractive to those who expect to submit high claims, the insurance company may decide to set its premiums a little higher than average to protect itself. The higher premiums may scare away some potential clients who do not expect to receive enough benefits to justify the premium. As a result, the customer base for the policy will tend even more toward those individuals who will make high claims, and the company is likely to respond by charging even higher premiums. Eventually, as the customer base grows smaller and more risky, the insurance company may withdraw the health insurance product entirely.

Much of the regulation to offset problems caused by imperfect information is legal in nature. In cases where there is asymmetric information that is known to one party but not to another party in a transaction, laws can place responsibility on the first party to make sure the other party receives the information in an understandable format. For example, truth-in-lending laws require that those making loans clearly disclose key provisions of the loan, to the degree of requiring the borrower to put initials beside written statements. The Sarbanes-Oxley law, created following the Enron crisis, places requirements on the conduct of corporations and their auditing firms to try to limit the potential for moral hazard.

When one party in an exchange defrauds another party by providing a good or service that is not what was promised, the first party can be fined or sued for its failure to protect against the outcomes to the other party. For example, if a firm sells a defective product that causes harm to the buyer, the firm that either manufactured or sold the item to the buyer could be held liable.

A defective product may be produced and sold because the safety risk is either difficult for the buyer to understand or not anticipated because the buyer is unaware of the potential. Governments may impose safety standards and periodic inspections on producers even though those measures would not have been demanded by the buyer. In extreme cases, the government may direct a seller to stop selling a good or service.

Other regulatory options involve equipping the ignorant party with better information. Government agencies can offer guidance in print or on Internet websites. Public schools may be required to make sure citizens have basic financial skills and understand the risks created by consumption of goods and services to make prudent decisions.

Where adverse selection discourages the operations of markets, regulation may be created to limit the liability to the parties involved. Individuals and businesses may be required to purchase or sell a product like insurance to increase and diversify the pool of exchanges and, in turn, to reduce the risk of adverse selection and make a market operable.

Limitations of Market Regulation

Although regulation offers the possibility of addressing market failure and inefficiencies that would not resolve by themselves in an unregulated free market economy, regulation is not easy or cost free.

Regulation requires expertise and incurs expenses. Regulation incurs a social transaction cost for market exchanges that is borne by citizens and the affected parties. In some instances, the cost of the regulation may be higher than the net efficiency gains it creates. Just as there are diminishing returns for producers and consumers, there are diminishing returns to increased regulation, and at some point the regulation becomes too costly.

Regulators are agents who become part of market transactions representing the government and people the government serves. Just as market participants deal with imperfect information, so do regulators. As such, regulators can make errors.

In our discussions about economics of organization in chapter 5, we noted that economics has approached the problem of motivating workers using the perspective that the workers' primary goal is their own welfare, not the welfare of the business that hires them. Unfortunately, the same may be said about regulators. Regulators may be enticed to design regulatory actions that result in personal gain rather than what is best for society as a whole in readjusting the market. For example, a regulator may go soft on an industry in hope of getting a lucrative job after leaving public service. In essence, this is another case of moral hazard. One solution might be to create another layer of regulation to regulate the regulators, but this adds to the expense and is likely self-defeating.

When regulation assumes a major role in a market, powerful sellers or buyers are not likely to treat the regulatory authority as an outside force over which they have no control. Often, these powerful parties will try to influence the regulation via lobbying. Aside from diminishing the intent of outside regulation, these lobbying efforts constitute a type of social waste that economists call *influence costs*, which are economically inefficient because these efforts represent the use of resources that could otherwise be redirected for production of goods and services.

One theory about regulation, called the *capture theory of regulation*,[4] postulates that government regulation is actually executed so as to improve the conditions for the parties being regulated and not necessarily to promote the public's interest in reducing market failure and market inefficiency. For example, in recent years there has been a struggle between traditional telephone service providers and cable television service providers. Each side wants to enter the market of the other group yet expects to maintain near monopoly power in its traditional market, and both sides pressure regulators to support their positions. In some cases, it has been claimed that the actual language of regulatory laws was proposed by representatives for the very firms that would be subject to the regulation.

Notes

Chapter 2

1. The particulars on depreciation can be found in any financial accounting text.

2. Readers interested in estimating the opportunity cost of investment capital are encouraged to consult a general text in financial analysis, such as Brigham and Ehrhardt (2010).

3. Many accounting and economics texts discuss the concept of discounting of profits over time. One good discussion can be found in an appendix in Hirschey and Pappas (1996).

4. A classic text in cost-benefit analysis was written by E. J. Mishan (1976).

Chapter 3

1. See Varian (1993) for a discussion of the substitution effect, income effect, and Giffen goods.

2. Bounded rationality and satisficing are discussed in Simon (1997).

3. Kotler and Armstrong (2010) is a popular text on marketing principles.

4. Stock and Watson (2007) is an established econometrics text.

5. One business forecasting text is a book authored by Hanke and Wichern (2009).

Chapter 4

1. Two classic texts on cost accounting and operations management are by Horngren (1972) and Stevenson (1986), respectively.

2. Stevenson (1986) addresses this approach to production planning extensively.

3. Wernerfelt (1984) wrote one of the key initial papers on the resource-based view of management.

4. The economics of learning by doing was introduced by Arrow (1962).

Chapter 5

1. A nice discussion of double marginalization appears in Shugart, Chappell, and Cottle (1994).

2. The best-selling book by Womack, Jones, and Roos (1990) describes the just-in-time philosophy.

3. Nobel laureate George Akerlof (1970) wrote a seminal paper examining adverse selection in the context of used cars.

4. See the text by Brickley, Smith, and Zimmerman (2001) for more about the free rider problem in economics of organizations.

5. The concept of cash-cow businesses is an aspect of the Boston Consulting Group matrix for corporate strategy (1970).

6. The initial article that stimulated later development of the transaction cost concept was by Ronald Coase (1937).

7. See Milgrom and Roberts (1992).

8. A good description of the informativeness principle appears in Samuelson and Marks (2010).

9. Nobel laureate Michael Spence (1974) introduced the economics of signaling.

10. See Milgrom and Roberts (1992).

Chapter 6

1. See Smith (1776).

2. The monopolistic competition model is discussed in Samuelson and Marks (2010).

3. The key text on the contestable market model is by Baumol, Panzar, and Willig (1982).

4. A good account of airline industry deregulation is in chapter 9 of Brock (2009).

5. See Porter (1980).

Chapter 7

1. See U.S. Census Bureau (2010).

2. A text that applies game theory to management is Brandenburger and Nalebuff (1996).

3. The durable goods problem is discussed in Kreps (2004).

Chapter 8

1. See Coase (1960).
2. Public goods are discussed in Baye (2010).
3. See Shapiro and Varian (1999).
4. The capture theory of regulation was introduced by Stigler (1971).

References

Akerlof, G. A. (1970). The market for "lemons": Quality, uncertainty, and the market mechanism. *Quarterly Journal of Economics 84*(3), 488–500.

Arrow, K. J. (1962). The economic implications of learning by doing. *Review of Economic Studies 29*(3), 155–173.

Baumol, W. J., Panzar, J. C., & Willig, R. J. (1982). *Contestable markets and the theory of industry structure.* San Diego, CA: Harcourt Brace Jovanovich.

Baye, M. R. (2010). *Microeconomics and business strategy.* New York, NY: McGraw-Hill Irwin.

Boston Consulting Group. (1970). *The product portfolio.* Retrieved December 13, 2010, from http://www.bcg.com/documents/file13255.pdf.

Brandenburger, A. M., & Nalebuff, B. J. (1996). *Co-opetition.* New York, NY: Currency Doubleday.

Brickley, J. A., Smith, C. W., Jr., & Zimmerman, J. L. (2001). *Managerial economics and organizational architecture.* New York, NY: McGraw-Hill Irwin.

Brigham, E. F., & Ehrhardt, M. C. (2010). *Financial management: Theory and practice* (13th ed.). Mason, OH: South-Western Cengage Learning.

Brock, J. W. (2009). *The structure of American industry* (12th ed.). Upper Saddle River, NJ: Pearson Prentice Hall.

Coase, R. H. (1937). The nature of the firm. *Economica 4*(16), 386–405.

Coase, R. H. (1960). The problem of social cost. *The Journal of Law and Economics 3*, 1–44.

Hanke, J. E., & Wichern, D. W. (2009). *Business forecasting* (9th ed.). Upper Saddle River, NJ: Pearson Prentice Hall.

Hirschey, M., & Pappas, J. L. (1996). *Managerial economics* (8th ed.). Fort Worth, TX: The Dryden Press.

Horngren, C. T. (1972). *Cost accounting: A managerial emphasis* (3rd ed.). Englewood Cliffs, NJ: Prentice Hall.

Kotler, P., & Armstrong, G. (2010). *Principles of marketing* (13th ed.). Upper Saddle River, NJ: Pearson Prentice Hall.

Kreps, D. M. (2004). *Microeconomics for managers.* New York, NY: W. W. Norton & Company.

Milgrom, P. R., & Roberts, J. (1992). *Economics, organization & management.* Englewood Cliffs, NJ: Prentice Hall.

Mishan, E. J. (1976). *Cost-benefit analysis.* New York, NY: Praeger.

Porter, M. E. (1980). *Competitive strategy.* New York, NY: The Free Press.

Samuelson, W. F., & Marks, S. G. (2010). *Managerial economics* (6th ed.). Hoboken, NJ: John Wiley & Sons.

Shapiro, C., & Varian, H. R. (1999). *Information rules.* Boston, MA: Harvard Business School Press.

Shugart, W. F., II, Chappell, W. F., & Cottle, R. L. (1994). *Modern managerial economics: Economic theory for business decisions.* Cincinnati, OH: South-Western Publishing Company.

Simon, H. A. (1997). *Administrative behavior* (4th ed.). New York, NY: The Free Press.

Smith, A. (1776). *The wealth of nations.* New York, NY: Modern Library.

Spence, A. M. (1974). *Market signaling.* Cambridge, MA: Harvard University Press.

Stevenson, W. J. (1986). *Production/operations management* (2nd ed.). Homewood, IL: Irwin.

Stigler, G. J. (1971). The theory of economic regulation. *Bell Journal of Economics and Management Science 2*(1), 3–21.

Stock, J. H., & Watson, M. W. (2007). *Introduction to econometrics* (2nd ed.). Boston, MA: Addison-Wesley.

U.S. Census Bureau. (2010). *Concentration ratios.* Retrieved December 13, 2010, from http://www.census.gov/econ/concentration.html.

Varian, H. A. (1993). *Intermediate microeconomics* (3rd ed.). New York, NY: W. W. Norton & Company.

Wernerfelt, B. (1984). A resource-based view of the firm. *Strategic Management Journal 5*(2), 171–180.

Womack, J. P., Jones, D. T., & Roos, D. (1990). *The machine that changed the world.* New York, NY: Rawson Associates Scribner.

Index

Note: The italicized *f* and *t* following page numbers refer to figures and tables, respectively.

Announcing the Business Expert Press Digital Library

Concise E-books Business Students Need for Classroom and Research

This book can also be purchased in an e-book collection by your library as

- a one-time purchase,
- that is owned forever,
- allows for simultaneous readers,
- has no restrictions on printing, and
- can be downloaded as PDFs from within the library community.

Our digital library collections are a great solution to beat the rising cost of textbooks. e-books can be loaded into their course management systems or onto student's e-book readers.

The **Business Expert Press** digital libraries are very affordable, with no obligation to buy in future years.

For more information, please visit **www.businessexpert.com/libraries**. To set up a trial in the United States, please contact **Sheri Allen** at *sheri.allen@globalepress.com*; for all other regions, contact **Nicole Lee** at *nicole.lee@igroupnet.com*.

OTHER TITLES IN OUR MANAGERIAL ECONOMICS COLLECTION

Working With Economic Indicators: Interpretation and Sources by Donald N. Stengel and Priscilla Chaffe-Stengel

Using Economic Data for Personal and Corporate Decision Making: What Have We Learned From California? by Phillip J. Romero

CPSIA information can be obtained at www.ICGtesting.com
Printed in the USA
BVOW010645131011

273529BV00005B/23/P

9 781606 492192